THE
Viking Jews

THE
Viking Jews
A HISTORY OF THE JEWS OF DENMARK

by
Ib Nathan Bamberger

SONCINO PRESS, LTD
New York

ISBN 1-871055-60-1
Copyright © 1983 by Ib Nathan Bamberger

All rights reserved

Soncino Press, Ltd.
123 Ditmas Avenue
Brooklyn, NY 11218

Printed in the United States of America

Contents

	Preface	
	Introduction	11
I	Earliest Immigration	19
II	Settlement in Danish Cities	28
III	Era of Transition, 1784-1814	33
IV	The Royal Decree of 1814	50
V	The Jewish Community and Its Institutions	65
VI	Meir Goldschmidt and His Period	79
VII	Interfaith Marriage	94
VIII	The Period after 1849	101
IX	East European Immigration at the Turn of the Century	114
X	German Immigration to Denmark	118
XI	The Occupation	130
XII	October 1943	138
	The Danish Kings	148
	Rabbis Officiating in Copenhagen	149
	Appendix I	150
	Appendix II	151
	Appendix III	154
	Bibliography-Notes	158

To the memory of
King Christian X
a truly righteous gentile

Preface to the Second Edition
1940–1990

The destruction of European Jewry during the second world war still staggers the imagination. Six million men, women and children were brutally murdered in the course of a few years, simply because they were what they were. As the lights of decency and humanity were extinguished in Europe, one country, under German occupation, reached out to save its Jewish citizens. That country was little Denmark!

The Viking Jews tells the story of a small group of Jews living in one of the smallest countries in Europe. These Jews were almost unknown to the rest of the world until the dark days of World War II, when the heroic acts of the Danish people saved them from the Nazi terror. Thus, Denmark became a universal symbol of courage and hope.

The Jews were first invited to Denmark by King Christian IV on November 25, 1622. Their history demonstrated the struggle to secure civil, political and economic equality with other Danes—a struggle which culminated in the royal decree of 1814, a most liberal document for that time.

The Jews' success in regard to rights stemmed from their ability to blend into Danish society at large without giving up their particular identity. The statistical data shows that the birth and mortality rate, educational level, and financial status of the Jewish community did not vary significantly from the rest of the Danish population. But this very congeniality between the Jews and the Danes led to the widespread problem of interfaith marriage which today threatens the survival of the Jewish community *as* Jewish.

Portraits are presented of outstanding individual Danish Jews—notably, the novelist and satirist Meir Goldschmidt, who took on Søren Kierkegaard and made all Copenhagen laugh at the celebrated philosopher; and the novelist, Georg Brandes, who considered himself a citizen of the world and rejected political Zionism as a "failure."

The final chapter of this book begins on the fateful day fifty years ago, April 9, 1940, when Denmark was occupied by the Germans. Danish Jews did not believe they would share the terrible fate of Jews in other European countries. They took their strength and security from observing the noble and beloved King Christian X riding daily, unguarded, through the streets of Copenhagen. In the summer of 1943, when acts of sabotage caused the Danish government to resign and the king to become a virtual prisoner in his castle, the Jews found themselves in a most precarious situation. The chapter climaxes with the miraculous escape of Danish Jewry.

In Denmark, as in almost no other European country, there never was a ghetto or a special street reserved for the Jews. On the contrary. The assimilation of Jews into Danish society progressed from the beginning, with particular rapidity in the last hundred years. Not until the rise of Nazism did a "Jewish problem" come into existence in Denmark. Even so, it must be said that most Danes had only scorn and contempt for anti-Jewish parties and ideologies—an attitude which prevails up to this day.

Out of a personal sense of debt to the Danish people for the help and kindness they extended to me and my people, especially during the dark days of 1943, this book was written. When we fled from Copenhagen in October 1943 there were so many individuals—whose names I do not know, from all walks of life: doctors, nurses, students, policemen, teachers, farmers, fishermen, bus drivers—who in their magnificent display of concern risked their own lives in order to save their Jewish fellow man. That display of loyalty, consideration and anxiety remains unmatched by any other European nation.

Recalling the heroic action taken by the Danes during the dark days of October, we are eternally grateful that the German actions did not deter them. With efforts unequalled by any other nation, the Danes insured the lives and the property of the Jews all through the remaining years of war. Totally unexpected was our welcome in May 1945: returning to Copenhagen, we found our homes in the same condition as we had left them. No vandalism, pilfering or theft occurred while we were in Sweden.

My good friends Milton and Esther Ackerman and their children, Tova, Sara, Sima and Avi have dedicated this work to the memory of their parents and grandparents o.b.m., Laszlo (Avrohom ben Naftoli Zvi) and Nancy (Malka bas Meir Yaacov) Ackerman, proud Jews who survived the terrible war years in concentration camp. Their devotion, attachment and love for the Jewish people, and their faith, stand as a proud symbol and eternal memorial. They imbued their children with traditional Jewish values which will always be a source of confidence and strength.

May this second edition of *The Viking Jews,* the story of the Danish Jews and their miraculous escape, be an inspiration for other nations in the future, to show them how to act to help those who truly are in need.

I.N.B.

New York, Spring 1990

Introduction

The kingdom of Denmark, the smallest of the Scandinavian countries, is also one of the smallest countries in Europe. With a population of approximately four million people, Denmark is composed of some five hundred islands, of which Zealand, with the capital city, Copenhagen, is the largest. To the north and east are Norway and Sweden. In the west is "mainland" Jutland. In the south, Jutland shares a common border with Germany. Denmark has a coast line more than 5000 miles long. It is a flat country, without mountains or canyons. Villages and hamlets dot the landscape. This pleasant country has been the home of the astronomer, Tycho Brahe; the author of world-famous fairy tales, Hans Christian Andersen, the nuclear physicist, Niels Bohr, and the performer, Victor Borge.

The Danes have a long and proud history. To understand this history one must comprehend the characteristics of the typical Dane. Self-confidence and self-reliance coupled with dry humor and a sincere interest in good food are his most evident traits. And the Dane has a liking for peace. He harbors no great ambition to conquer the world or outer space.—"To remain on the ground serves us best" is a common saying in Denmark.

The Dane detests war of any kind. In international disputes he prefers to remain strictly neutral. He is not infused with religious fervor. Denmark adopted the Lutheran religion very early after the Reformation as the state religion, but gave religious liberty to all its citizens. This privilege has always been scrupulously observed.

Before the seventeenth century Jews were not permitted to enter the kingdom of Denmark, but they had little interest in going there, anyway, because Denmark was located away from the main routes of commercial travel. No raw materials were to be found in the country. No precious metals or valuable objects were obtainable there. Denmark was known mainly for its dairy products.

In the seventeenth century, as the Church's influence declined, nationalism became a potent force in western Europe. In Amsterdam, one of the great centers of commerce, a number of Jews were engaged in business. It began to be observed that these Jews and their participation in commercial enterprises contributed to the prosperity of Holland. Other western countries wanted to share in this prosperity, Denmark among them. And so King Christian IV invited certain Sephardic Jews to settle within the Danish borders.

Greatly beloved by the citizens of Denmark, Christian was a man of foresight, vision and imagination. One of his desires was to beautify the city of Copenhagen. He embarked upon an elaborate project to erect buildings which still stand today. The Round Tower, which served as his astronomical observatory, the Rosenborg Castle, which houses the crown jewels, the stock exchange, and a number of churches and other buildings all bear testimony to his activities and accomplishments.

Soon after their arrival in Copenhagen, the new Jewish immigrants encountered the preachings of Holger Paulli. Paulli was a Danish religious fanatic who traveled in Europe and North Africa, demanding that Jews convert to Christianity in order to speed the second coming of the Messiah. In 1706 he returned to Copenhagen and gathered Jews in his home for the purpose of preaching. King Frederick IV did not appreciate Paulli and ordered the police chief of Copenhagen to prevent his further proselytizing activities. The king feared that Paulli would so arouse the Christian population against the Jews that riots would result. Afterwards, Paulli published a few articles and pamphlets, but he discontinued his missionary work, and the Jews had peace.

The arrival of Ashkenazic Jews in Denmark resulted in a certain amount of friction, but these two groups realized early the necessity of working together in harmony and peace. They united in all religious, social and economic endeavors, and this unity has remained until the present time.

The condition of the early settlers in Copenhagen is described in much detail by Glückel of Hameln in her memoirs. She tells about Abraham Cantor, her first manservant: "We had him to look after the children. Later he left us for some years and went into a little business of his own. . . . We advanced him money and sent him to Copenhagen and today it is said he is a man worth 10,000 Reichsthaler or more."[1] Cantor was among the very first Jews to come to Copenhagen. Born in Hildesheim, and therefore sometimes referred to as Abraham Hildesheim, he obtained royal permission to deal in jewelry and clothing in 1683 and died in 1715.

A brother, Axel Cantor, is mentioned on a tax list dated 1678. Axel obtained citizenship on December 9, 1691. His son-in-law, David Israel, who died as a young man, was the first to be buried in the Jewish cemetery in Møllegade, Copenhagen on September 5, 1693.

Two children of Glückel married Danish Jews. Nathan Guldsmed, her oldest son, married Miriam Ballin. In 1704 Nathan received permission to settle in Copenhagen. He engaged extensively in commerce. He died at an old age on March 12, 1744. His last name, Goldschmidt, always appears in the Danish form of Guldsmed.

His younger brother Just or Jost (Josef) Goldschmidt was married to a daughter of Mayer Goldschmidt. Glückel tells us about her journey to this wedding. On May 6, 1699, Just received royal permission to settle in Copenhagen on condition that he pay an annual sum of 50 Reichsthaler to the royal treasury until he built a house. In return, he was held free from all other taxes. He was a jeweler and dealt also in promissory notes. He died about 1734.

Both sons of Glückel of Hameln as well as Abraham Cantor appear on a tax list, dated 1710.[2]

On June 19, 1630, King Christian IV proclaimed that no Jew under fifteen years of age could be baptized, even if he consented to

---

[1] Beth Zion Abrahams (translator and editor) *The Life of Glückel of Hameln*, (New York: Horovitz Publishing Co. 1963) pp. 40, 68.

[2] Julius Salomon og Josef Fisher, *Mindeskrift i Anledning of Hundredaarsdagen for Anordningen af 29 Marts 1814* (København: J. Jørgensen & Co. 1914), p. 121, note 4.

be of his own free will. Moreover, should any Jew decide at a more mature age to convert to Christianity, the Church had to give him forty days for reconsideration.

The first Jew to be baptized in Denmark was Daniel Salomon. He was a Polish Jew who converted in 1620 in Copenhagen in Vor Frue Kirke. The ceremony was scheduled for October 31. Such great masses of people gathered to witness this momentous event that it had to be postponed to the next day.

Another conversion, which took place in Frederiksberg Kirke in 1688, was accompanied with great pomp and ceremony. Members of the royal court, ministers, high church officials and other dignitaries were in attendance. The officiating priest noted in the church registry that there were "no less than seven godfathers—unknown to me—but all members of the royal court." Obviously, the convert was a man of means. The poorer Jews present were embarrassed and confused by the assembled dignitaries. "This is not the way to fulfill our sacred mission," concludes the officiating priest in his remarks.[3] Bishop Balle, who was known as a friend of the Jews, noted pointedly that "it has become clear that proselytes are individuals of which Christianity has no great joy and very little honor."

One of the last missionary activities against the Jews involved a public collection of money in 1754. The appeal was made in all the churches of Denmark and Norway and yielded 1,440 Reichsthaler. But the money was never used for the purpose it had been raised, since no candidates for conversion came forward. By the year 1800 that capital had grown to 5,516 Reichsthaler. On the advice of Bishop Balle the fund was abolished and the money transferred to a new fund for retired teachers' widows.[4]

In 1729 there was great excitement in Copenhagen; the city sheriff, Jens Gedelock, had converted to Judaism. Gedelock was displeased with the quarreling among the Christian sects and suspected that they were all mistaken in their beliefs. Only the late descendants of the patriarchs, the Jews, were correct in their faith, he believed. On his deathbed, he was visited by a priest who came to win

[3] Benjamin Balslev, *De Danske Jøders Historie*, (Copenhagen: O. Lohse, 1932), p.26.
[4] *Ibid.* p.29.

him back to Christianity. But he refused, whereupon the priest submitted his soul to the devil. Jens was, nevertheless, secretly buried in a Christian cemetery. When, some time later, this became known, his body was exhumed to be reinterred in the Jewish cemetery. But some Jews objected to this, because Jens was not circumcised. It was an insult to the Jews and their burial ground to have such an individual lying there. The case was brought before the king, who permitted the body to be removed from its second grave and buried outside the gates.[5]

The threads of tolerance, accommodation and mutual concern visible in these early encounters evolved into a pattern of relationship between native Danes and Jews which persisted into later times. So firmly established did this pattern become that, as we shall see, Danish Jews were able to resist Jewish reform movements from the south, which sprang from altogether different conditions.

Once acculturated to Danish ways and thinking, the Jews in Denmark did all in their power to become an integral part of the country's population. As soon as they were able, the Jewish immigrants tried to speak Danish, live like the Danes and adopt Danish values consistent with their religion.

In Denmark, one does not break with tradition but maintains it at all cost. In regard to German religious influences, one must bear in mind that Denmark and Germany had been at war many times on account of Slesvig-Holstein. A certain animosity towards Germany was always present in Denmark. Political and cultural experience taught one to be on guard against anything German. This explains, to a large degree, the Danish Jews' resistance to the German-Jewish reform movement of mid-nineteenth century, including prayers and hymns in German. To be German in Denmark has never been a mark of distinction.

The affectionate relationship between Danes and Jews was bound to test the faithfulness of the latter to their beliefs and peoplehood. Interfaith marriages, to be discussed later, affected a large number of Danish Jews. But at the same time a nucleus of practicing Danish Jews always remained. These were opposed to interfaith

[5] *Ibid.* p.27.

marriages on religious grounds. Tradition, whether secular or religious, is part of Danish thinking and philosophy.

For their part, Danish Christians continued to honor their traditions of tolerance and freedom, so that by 1814 Jews were able to gain complete political, social and economic equality.[6] In the admirable history of Danish Jewry, one cannot overlook the Danes' strong humanistic values, their sense of decency, and their care for all citizens. These characteristics gave them confidence in all their undertakings, belief in their own worth, a sense of responsibility towards their fellow human beings and respect for the dignity of the human soul.

But now it is time to look at these facts, developments and events in detail.

---

[6] Raphael Edelman, "David Simonsen," *Ved 150 Aars-Dagen for Anordningen af 29 Marts 1814*, ed. Julius Margolinsky og Poul Meyer (København: A/S Oscar Fraenckel & Co., 1964), p.110.

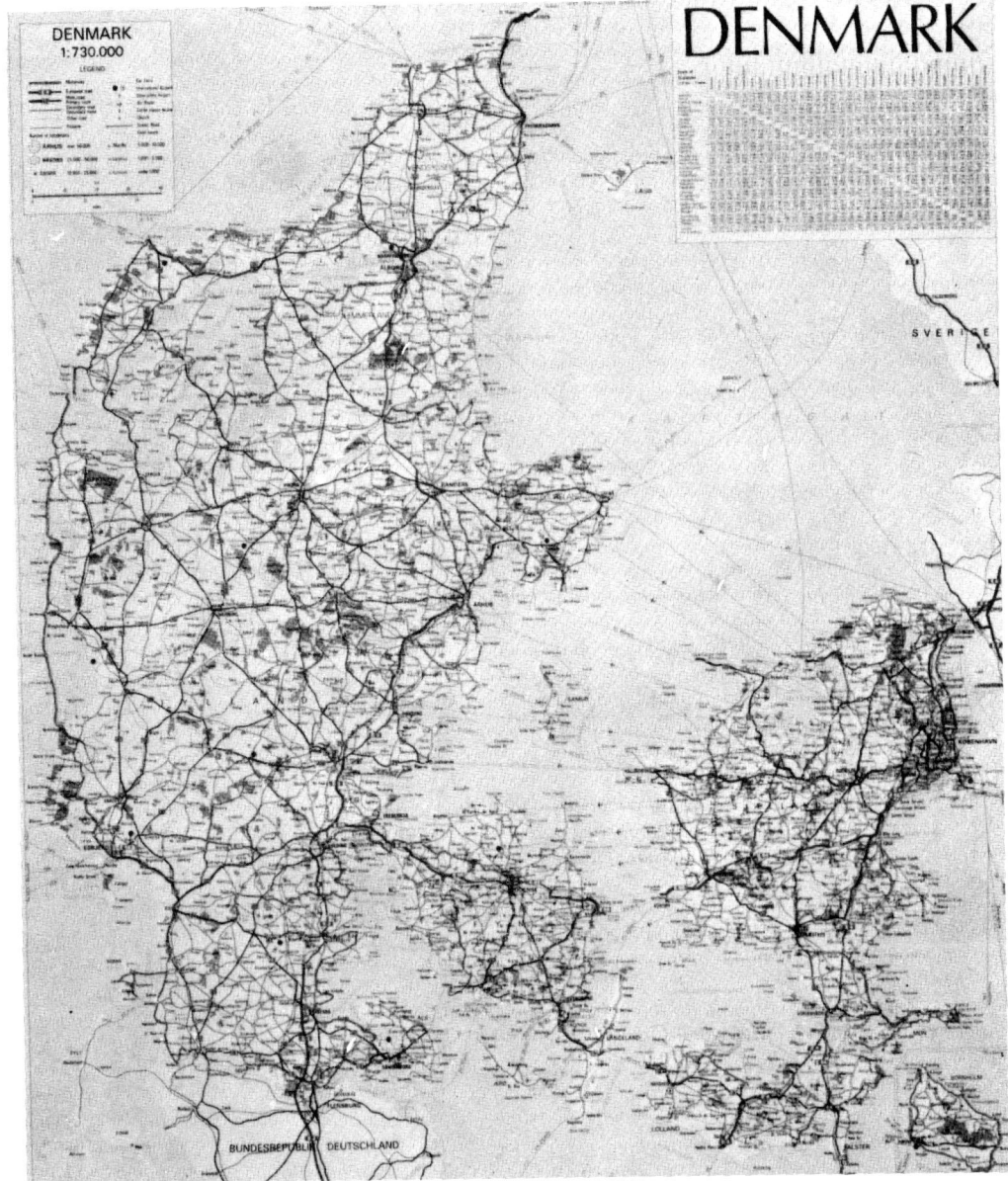

I

Earliest Immigration

The earliest recorded Jewish settlement within the Danish kingdom was in the city of Altona and its suburb Ottensen.[1]

Altona, with the adjacent cities Hamburg and Wandsbeck, formed the famous Jewish community 'AHU'. Only Altona, however, was situated in Holstein within the Danish border of Southern Jutland.

The political history of Southern Jutland, which consisted of the two duchies, Slesvig and Holstein, dates back to antiquity. The political, social and cultural development of this area was marked by long and bitter struggles. In 1475 the Danish king, Christian I, was elected duke of Slesvig and Holstein. The various estates in Slesvig-Holstein still retained the right, however, to elect a successor to the king, provided he be of royal blood, and that the two lands, Slesvig and Holstein, should remain forever indivisible. This somewhat peculiar latter requirement became the bone of contention between Denmark and the German states for centuries. In the late Middle Ages the Danish crown-estates in Holstein were given to German dukes. The nobility influenced the citizens of Holstein to develop a strong nationalistic feeling for Germany. Slesvig, however, remained more Danish. Nevertheless, both Slesvig and Holstein were

---

[1] Julius Salomon og Josef Fischer, *Mindeskrift i Anledning af Hundredaarsdagen for Anordningen af 29 Marts 1814* (København: J. Jørgensen & Co. 1914) p.29.

more or less united with Denmark since the Middle Ages, usually with a Danish king as duke. The twin duchies were taken from Denmark in 1864 and incorporated into the German federation of states. But in 1920, after a plebiscite, Slesvig was divided into North and South Slesvig, the former reincorporated into Denmark, the latter retained by Germany. Thus Altona was a Danish city until 1864. The importance of this fact was that the rabbis elected to Altona had to be authorized by the Danish kings.

At the time Jews first settled there—by permission of King Frederick II in 1584—Altona belonged to the Duke of Schaumburg, whose duchy was a part of Denmark. These newcomers were granted the status of *Schutzjuden*, protected Jews.[2] A tombstone, dated 1621, over the grave of Samuel son of Judah, founder of the Altona congregation, is the earliest record of Jews in Denmark.[3]

In 1620, King Christian IV (1588-1648) founded the city-fortress of Glückstadt in Holstein. As it was a practice in those days, the king extended an invitation to the Portuguese Jews of Amsterdam and Hamburg to settle in this newly founded city. (See Appendix I.) The invitation was issued in Haderslev on November 25, 1622. The king promised certain privileges in regard to freedom of religion and commerce. He furthermore invited one or two representatives of the people[4] to inspect the living condition in Glückstadt. The royal invitation mentions the master of the mint as well as Albertus Dionys as his negotiators.[5] The king's hope was that Glückstadt (Denmark) would challenge Hamburg (Germany) in commerce and industry. But this scheme did not succeed. Neither did Glückstadt become the center of Jewish settlement, but rather Altona; nor was Glückstadt able to challenge Hamburg.

Christian IV ratified the privileges for the Jews in a decree of Au-

---

[2] Benjamin Balslev, *De Danske Jøders Historie*, (Copenhagen: O. Lohse, 1932) p.4.
[3] Julius Salomon og Josef Fischer, p.29.
[4] It is interesting to note that the word 'Jew' does not appear in the royal invitation at all.
[5] Shimon Altshul in *Dos Wochenblat* gives the names of the first Jews who settled in Glückstadt: Cornelius Jansen, Moshe Gideon Abudienti and Abraham de Fonseca.

gust 1, 1641.⁶ This document consisted of eleven points dealing with specific regulations. The Jews were permitted to have a synagogue, conduct religious services according to their ritual and bury their dead in a separate cemetery according to Jewish rites. The rabbi, cantor and sexton were exempted from all taxes. Children upon leaving their parental home had to pay a fee for royal protection. Jews were permitted to engage in all lawful business and commerce, and slaughter animals according to Jewish law (*sh'chita*). They were permitted to collect one pfenning on each Mark as interest per week. They had to return pledged objects within six weeks without collecting interest. They had to return stolen objects to their rightful owners if they had bought these objects under false assumption. To promote the welfare of the country and to eliminate damages and losses, they had to pay the royal protection fee at the appropriate time (Easter). Finally they were prohibited from granting foreigners (Jews) residence in their homes without official permission. This document which is extremely important, provided the Jewish immigrants with a basis for settlement and earning a livelihood. The stipulation regarding their religious laws was most liberal, considering the time when the decree was issued.

In the same year (1641), Christian IV gave the Jews permission to establish a congregation and build a synagogue.⁷ Among the first Jews residing in Altona, there were a few who came in close contact with the royal court. Gabriel Gometz provided the king with arms, jewelry and precious silks. Don Manuel Texeira of Hamburg was an important merchant who traveled extensively in Denmark and Norway. Samuel de Lima (or Limma) of Amsterdam and Hamburg, together with his brother Isak, supplied jewelry to king Frederick III. Throughout the reign of Christian IV a spirit of liberalism and understanding towards the Jews began to prevail.

It is during this time that some Jews settled in the capital city of Copenhagen. The first Jew invited there by King Christian IV, Dr.

---

⁶ This document, which was issued in Glückstadt, is quoted by Altschul (p.9) in the original German language. No source is given. I was unable to trace the source for this document in any other work.
⁷ Max Friediger, *Jødernes Historie*, (Copenhagen: P. Haase & Søns Forlag, 1934), p.331.

Jonah Charizi, lived on Østergade and died in Copenhagen in 1626. It is thought that when the king built the Round Tower in 1617, Dr. Charizi was instrumental in placing the Hebrew Tetragrammaton on the tower. Furthermore, in 1618, the king wrote to him that he should consider bringing in foreign capital for the East Asiatic company which at that time was experiencing great financial problems.[8]

The first Jewish person permanently residing in Copenhagen was Israel Salomon Levy. His name is registered on a war tax list of 1676. A list from 1682 contains the names of seven Jewish families consisting of 19 persons.[9] But these persons still needed permission to settle permanently in Denmark and this could only be obtained by a royal letter of protection. When a few poor Jews attempted to reside there without one, they were expelled. The requirement of a letter of protection was reaffirmed in decrees of 1678 and 1681 and in the Danish Constitution of 1683. When the law was interpreted to include also Portuguese Jews, a protest was registered by Diego Teixeira de Mattos, to whom the king owed a substantial amount of money. Thereupon a royal decree, dated July 30, 1684 was issued which reaffirmed the special privileges granted to Portuguese Jews.

Nevertheless, it was German Jews who were successful in establishing a Jewish community in Copenhagen. The royal jeweler, Israel David, and his partner, Meyer Goldschmidt, received royal permission on Dec. 16, 1684, to conduct in their homes "their devotions, mornings and evenings, and psalms, but without any sermons, in order not to offend anyone." David died at an early age in 1695 and was buried in Altona. Goldschmidt remained at the helm of the Jewish congregation until his death in 1736.

He became the only Jew in Denmark who ever faced a possible charge of ritual murder. He was a very wealthy and distinguished man who enjoyed many privileges. In 1699 a poor woman visited him and said she wanted to sell a child. She had heard that the Jews needed blood from a Christian child to prepare matzohs. Goldschmidt did the only wise thing. He went to the city sheriff,

---

[8] The name Copenhagen is sometimes spelled in Hebrew in one word, sometimes in two words, perhaps because originally the name was "Kjøbmands Havn" (the merchant's harbour).

[9] Salomon og Fischer, p.30.

who arrested and punished the woman. Never again were the Jews of Denmark associated with human blood. Religious services were conducted in Goldschmidt's home until 1732, when a house was rented in Laederstraede and a synagogue established on its first floor. The synagogue was moved several times, until finally, in 1743, a permanent site was bought in the same street. In 1795 this synagogue was consumed by a great fire that overtook the city. A request to rebuild it was granted on Aug. 26, 1799, but on condition that all other places of Jewish worship be incorporated into the new structure. Unfortunately it was impossible for the Sephardim and Ashkenazim to agree, and the building of the synagogue was postponed. The wars with England in 1801 and 1807 and the bombardment of Copenhagen by the British fleet brought the matter to a standstill.[10]

The growth of the Jewish community in Copenhagen was very slow. In 1694 we find 12 Jewish families residing there. These few Jews formed the nucleus of Jewish life in Denmark. The first rabbi to serve this tiny congregation was Abraham Solomon from Moravia, who was engaged in 1687. In 1693, a young man, David Israel, died and was buried outside the city walls. The land containing the burial place was bought the following year as a permanent cemetery. When Rabbi Solomon died on May 20, 1700, he was buried here. Known as the cemetery in Møllegade, this site still exists today. Rabbi Solomon's successor was Israel Behr, the author of *Ohel Yisroel*, who died in Fredericia in 1732.[11]

A tax list of the year 1711 contains the names of 36 Jewish men and women and 48 children. But these were only persons of means. Fortuneless Jews were not registered. It is estimated that Copenhagen had 65,000 citizens of whom 350 belonged to the "Jewish Nation" (.05%).[12]

In 1726 there were 65 Jewish families residing in Copenhagen. A census taken a few years afterwards (following a fire in 1728 which destroyed a great part of Copenhagen) showed that there were 91 Jewish men, 70 women and 170 children. The city government felt

[10] Salomon og Fischer, p.20.
[11] Friediger, p.334.
[12] Salomon og Fischer, p. 31.

that the Jewish population was increasing too rapidly and reported its fears to the chancellery. As a result, the government issued a decree stating that in the future no Jew be permitted to live in Copenhagen unless he was the actual owner of 1000 Rigsdaler.[13]

During the reign of Frederick IV (1699-1730) some feeble attempts were made by the Lutheran clergy to convert the Jews. In 1728 the officers of the Jewish congregation received a notice for the Jews to attend the Vajsenhus church service, where a priest was to instruct them in the teachings of Christianity. A strong protest was immediately offered, but before the ordinance actually became effective, a fire destroyed the church. The problem literally died in the flames and did not arise again.[14]

Approximately thirty years later, in 1760, the number of Jews increased considerably. The families living in Copenhagen were estimated as being between 130-140 (700 persons). Six years later (1766) the first synagogue in Laederstraede was dedicated. It had a capacity of 320 seats for both men and women.[15]

Twenty-four years later, we find the increase has continued. It is generally estimated that in the year 1784 Jewish families residing in Copenhagen numbered 250. At least 70 families received support from the Jewish community, 100 families were regarded as middle class (able to survive by strict economy) and the rest classified as well-to-do.

Gradually the Jews' position improved, and the growth of their population became proportional to that of the rest of the citizenry. In 1787, Copenhagen had approximately 90,000 people, of whom some 1,200 (250 families) were Jews (1.3%).[16]

In the year 1798 permission was granted for the first interfaith marriage to a Jewish man from Kalundborg who desired to marry a

---

[13] Steffen Linvald, "Den jødiske Frihedskamp i Danmark og Anordningen af 29 Marts 1814," *Ved 150 Aars-Dagen for Anordningen af 29 Marts 1814*, ed. Julius Margolinsky og Poul Meyer, (København: A/S Oscar Fraenckel & Co., 1964) p.14.

[14] Friediger, p.336.

[15] Julius Margolinsky, *Ligfølgeselskabet, Jødisk Broderselskab af 1768* (København: B. Nielsen's Eftf., 1967) p.8.

[16] Steffen Linvald, p.15.

non-Jewish woman. A condition was attached to the authorization, that the children born of the union would be raised in the Christian faith. The man, however, did not have to convert to Christianity.[17] In the same year, Jewish students were permitted to attend the University of Copenhagen without restriction. This was a signal advance. However, their opportunities to better their economic position after graduation remained few, although a royal resolution decreed that no discriminatory differences could be applied in hiring employees.[18]

The political situation in Europe at the beginning of the nineteenth century had considerable impact upon Denmark and the Jews living there. Napoleon's armies had conquered the greater part of Europe. For a long time Denmark adhered to a policy of strict neutrality. But, when in the year 1800, Denmark joined Russia in a coalition of neutrality, England sent its navy to Denmark to force it out of the coalition. The attack came as a surprise. The Danish navy was completely unprepared, and the *Slaget paa Rheden* on April 2, 1801, was won by England. In 1807 the British attacked once again, bombarded Copenhagen and captured the fleet. Fires destroyed numerous buildings, among them the synagogue and the school. New taxes had to be levied. Some of the Portuguese Jews refused to shoulder the obligation, but a court decided against them. As a result, 330 members of the Jewish community in Copenhagen were taxed, whereas 170 were excused because of poverty. There were now 500 Jewish families residing in Copenhagen in the year 1807.[19]

In 1813 a literary attack upon the Jews became a major issue and threatened all the gains which had been made up to then. The poet Thomas Thaarup translated and published a pamphlet *Moses og Jesus* by the German writer Frederich Buchholz (1803) into Danish. The pamphlet discussed the Jewish people, its history and religion in a context rife with hate and anti-Semitic remarks. Thaarup provided a preface in which he stated that neither the translation nor

---

[17] Salomon og Fischer, p.54. Cf. chapter VII.
[18] *Ibid.* p.23.
[19] *Ibid.* p.61.

his preface (which amplified the remarks of Buchholz) were motivated by hatred of the Jews. His purpose was only to expose the truth. He would be happy, he wrote, if the theories and allegations against the Jews in the pamphlet could be refuted.

Many prominent individuals, including the poet Baggesen of Kiel and Steen Steensen Blicher of Randlev (both Christians) as well as C. N. David, who later became finance minister and M. L. Nathanson (both Jews), accepted the challenge.[20] The dispute, which in the beginning had a purely academic tone, soon attacked the position of the Jews in Denmark and their civil and political rights, with the royal confessor, Dr. Bastholm, joining in the attack on the Jews.

Basically, the allegations against the Jews in Denmark boiled down to the charge that they had exported money out of the country and thus caused a financial crisis. Representatives of the Jewish community responded with a document refuting this. The document contained the following statistical information about Danish Jews. A total of 2,400 Jews resided in Copenhagen. Seven hundred forty were adult men, 25 of whom were merchants, 50 students, artisans and teachers, and about 240 members of the armed forces, including the navy.[21]

Numerous writings both for and against the Jews appeared, the most noteworthy being a pamphlet by Gottlieb Euchel entitled *Towards Eternal Peace* in which the Jewish author defended his coreligionists.

But Thaarup, who had started it all, wrote no further on the matter. If he had hoped that the government would enact laws of an anti-Jewish nature he was sorely disappointed. On the contrary, the government took the position that a need existed to provide greater protection and security for its Jewish citizens, so that such minor literary attacks upon Jews as had occurred would not be repeated in the future.

---

[20] Balslev, p.43.
[21] *Ibid*. p.44. Regarding the wealth of the Jews it is noteworthy that Marcus Rubin, chief of the department of taxation, director of the National Bank, historian and statistician (1854-1923) reported that Copenhagen in 1810 had 100 taxpayers, each earning more than 10.000 Rigsdaler. Of these, only six were Jews.

Moreover, the dispute—which lasted three years—resulted in a more tolerant general attitude towards the Jews. Throughout the episode, the defence had remained objective and reasonable, and the king, Frederick VI, had refused to be swayed by the attackers' literary arguments. His advisors were likewise unimpressed by the mountain of their writings. On March 29, 1814—a most joyous day for the Jews of Denmark—a royal decree was issued which stated that "those of the Jewish faith who were born in the kingdom of Denmark, or have received permission to settle within its borders, should have equal opportunity with the rest of the citizens to earn a living and support themselves according to the established laws."[22]

---

[22] The whole literary controversy is too broad a subject to be discussed here. A detailed account (in Danish) is found in *Musaeum for 1890* by Villads Christensen. Parts are also found in *Jøderne som Danske Borgere*, 1897.

II

Settlement in Danish Cities

When the Jews entered Denmark, they arrived mostly from the south, crossing the frontier between Germany and Jutland. They were always few in numbers. Primarily they came to make small business transactions or to peddle merchandise from foreign countries. Simon Hertvigsen obtained permission to settle in the city of Ribe, Jutland, in 1673, the same year Israel Fürst received permission to settle in Copenhagen. Consequently Ribe became the first real Danish provincial city in which Jews resided. But a noticeable change occurred in 1678. In that year, King Christian V (1670-1699) revoked the special privileges of Portuguese Jews. Henceforth the government restricted the immigration of Jews for settlement, except in the city of Fredericia.[1]

On March 11, 1682, Fredericia received the unique right to grant asylum to "all impoverished homeowners...and others who do not demand special title." Among those who had come to Fredericia prior to 1682 were a number of Jews, who took full advantage of this grant.[2]

In general, Jews residing in the provincial cities, did not engage in business in the city proper. They visited villages and hamlets,

[1] Benjamin Balslev, *De Danske Jøders Historie* (Copenhagen: O. Lohse, 1932), p.14.
[2] Julius Salomon og Josef Fischer, *Mindeskrift i Anledning af Hunredaarsdagen for Anordningen af 29 Marts 1814* (København: J. Jørgensen & Co. 1914), p.87.

especially on market days, where they offered for sale all types of merchandise from distant lands. The competition they offered native merchants led to the voicing of strong objections at the various city council meetings. In many cases the objections were sustained. In Aalborg, Aarhus, Odense and Viborg, Jews were denied permission to sell their goods to the nobility, proprietors, clergy or sheriffs. However, in the year 1725, eleven Jews of Fredericia petitioned the king to grant them these desirable markets. Attached to their petition was a certificate from the city council of Fredericia which stated that "the Jews are good and harmless citizens, who in times of war have contributed their best, as well as their share of taxes according to the royal demands and levied by the state." The request was thereupon granted on March 30, 1726.[3]

It should be noted that it was not humanitarian considerations alone that caused the Danish government to accede to the Jews. Economic conditions and considerations were far more important. When Jews settled in any provincial city, they tended to enhance the local economy. In cases where they infringed upon the economic well-being of the citizenry or were poor and sustained themselves primarily by peddling, they were, however, prone to expulsion. The city of Nakskov was originally settled by wealthy Portuguese Jews. Later, these Jews moved to other cities, leaving behind some poor German Jews. The municipal authorities, thereupon decided in 1751 that a total of four Jewish families would be sufficient for Nakskov and the rest were expelled.[4]

The small Jewish communities in the provincial Danish cities were active entities for almost two hundred years. Besides in Ribe, Fredericia and Nakskov, Jews resided in several other cities. The largest Jewish communities outside Copenhagen were in Randers, Fredericia and Aalborg which had, respectively, 194, 125 and 113 Jewish people. Eight cities had between 50 and 100 Jews—Helsingør, Slagelse, Odense, Assens, Svendborg, Viborg and Nakskov. Scattered over the rest of the country were 259 other Jews.

---

[3] Josef Fischer, *Slaegten Levin-Fredericia* (Copenhagen: Oscar Fraenkels Bogtrykkeri, 1916), p.8.
[4] Balslev, p.17.

The number of Jews in the aforementioned cities, which in the first census of the Jews (1834) had been 1,141, declined by 1890 to 360 individuals. Randers alone had 146 while the remaining cities showed a decrease from 947 to 214. This shrinkage continued until the beginning of the twentieth century, when these Jewish communities completely ceased to be. Randers, the longest surviving Jewish community, was officially closed down in 1945.[5]

While it lasted, the Jewish community of Fredericia had a healthy existence. Thus we find that a last will and testament of a printer of that city, J. M. Eibeschutz, drawn up on September 6, 1882, stipulated that from the interest of the estate 100 Kroner should be paid to the Jewish community every year. This amount was to be administered by the officers of the community and used for the expenses incurred by the synagogue or for the support and assistance of poor Jews who did not receive welfare form the public welfare fund. Furthermore, 200 Kroner annually were to be given to the (non-Jewish) workmen's guild, half for the old age fund, and half for the technical school in Fredericia. Finally, 50 Kroner were set aside to be used annually to help Jews of limited means pay for rent in Fredericia.[6]

Some of the smaller communities had rabbis. In Faaborg, L. M. Wallach was spiritual leader for nearly fifty years.[7] In Aalborg, where a Jewish community was established in 1854, Salomon Mielziner was rabbi for thirty-five years. His brother, Moses Mielziner, who came to Denmark from Waren in Mecklenburg in 1854, was rabbi in Randers, and in 1857 became the principal of the Jewish school in Copenhagen. While in Copenhagen, he submitted a doctoral dissertation to the university in Giessen, Germany, and was awarded a Ph.D. degree. The dissertation, published in 1859 by P. G. Phillipson, Copenhagen was entitled *Die Verhältnisse der Sklaven bei den alten Hebräern, nach Biblischen und talmudischen*

---

[5] Julius Margolinsky, "Det jødiske Folketal i Denmark efter 1814," *Ved 150 Aarsdagen for Anordningen af 29 Marts 1814*, ed. Julius Margolinsky og Poul Meyer (København: A/S Oscar Fraenkel & Co., 1964), p.201.

[6] *Tillaeg til Fortegnelser over de i det Mosaiske Troessamfund i Kjøbenhavn stiftede Legator* (Kjøbenhavn: O. C. Olsen & Co., 1890), pp. 49-50.

[7] Max Friediger, *Jødernes Historie* (Copenhagen: P. Haase & Søns Forlag, 1934), p.357.

Quellen dargestellt: Ein Beitrag zur hebräisch-jüdischen Alterturtumskunde. The book is dedicated to Moses Amsel Meyer from whose scholarship fund Mielziner had received aid for three years. In 1865 Mielziner went to the United States, and in 1879 he became professor of Talmud at the Hebrew Union College, Cincinnati, Ohio. Upon the death of Isac M. Weis on March 26, 1900, Mielziner became president of that institution, which office he held until his death in 1903.

Nevertheless, the inability of the provincial cities to provide for the social and religious needs of its Jewish citizens remained a problem. The movement of Jews to the capital city of Copenhagen in the nineteenth century began to accelerate. To find proper partners in the provinces for marriageable offspring became more and more difficult. Consequently a constant decrease of the Jewish provincial population was inevitable and could only end in the complete disappearance of the Jews from the smaller cities. The following table reveals this process in the most important cities.

Table 1[8]

Number of Jews living in Danish provincial cities according to census, 1834 - 1890

	1834	1850	1860	1880	1890
Elsinore	74	45	38	7	2
Slagelse	90	77	50	12	9
Nakskov	45	36	34	38	18
Assens	69	49	33	4	3
Faaborg	77	76	68	31	22
Odense	82	63	56	28	30
Aalborg	113	132	121	68	41
Horsens	68	60	88	68	35
Fredericia	125	98	96	39	41
Randers	194	185	200	172	146

[8] Balslev, p.93.

A census based on religion has not been permitted in Denmark in this century. However, it is not unreasonable to say that the few remaining Jews living outside of Copenhagen play no role in the development of Jewish life in that country today.

The only remnant left of the former provincial Jewish settlements are the cemeteries. These are supervised and administered by the Jewish community of Copenhagen. Thus, for all practical purposes, Jewish life in Denmark has become concentrated in Copenhagen, where all social, cultural and religious institutions necessary for the welfare of Danish Jewry have been developed.

III

Era of Transition, 1784-1814

The beginning of the change of condition for the Jews in Denmark must be dated from approximately 1784. Guldberg, the prime minister, had been deposed.[1] The crown prince (later King Frederick VI) became the ruling power of the country.[2] Frederick had the foresight to surround himself with men like A. P. Bernstoff,[3] the Reventlow brothers,[4] and C. Colbjørnsen.[5] The most im-

---

[1] Ove Høegh Guldberg, 1731-1808, was born in Horsens, Jutland; received an extensive education; became professor at the famous academy in Sorø, obtained position as tutor for the heir of the Danish throne; later became prime minister. Guldberg worked for the establishment of schools, improvements for native-born citizens and more Danish speaking at court, but was strictly opposed to any type of reforms for the benefit of peasant and farmers, who comprised the majority of the population.
[2] Christian VII, his father, was considered insane, and legally barred from ruling the country.
[3] Andreas Peter Bernstoff, 1735-1797, count and statesman, held various posts in the government, including that of secretary for foreign affairs. During the French-English war in 1777, he wanted Denmark to remain strictly neutral. He was most liberal minded in regard to the forthcoming emancipation of the farmers.
[4] Carl Frederick Reventlow, 1753-1834, count and statesman, held numerous diplomatic positions, as well as various positions at court. He was secretary of state 1797-1802.
 Ludwig Reventlow, 1751-1801, count and statesman, started reform work in various places and gained understanding and agreement among the peasants. He also started schools on his estates.
[5] Christian Colbjørnsen, 1749-1814, main organizer of various reform movements, was secretary of the committee for agrarian policy and a prime force behind the establishment of the 1788 Law of Emancipation and of freedom of the press in 1790.

portant task these men saw facing themselves was the emancipation of the peasants and the freeing of all serfs. This spirit of equality for all "stepchildren" of Danish society also embraced the Jews.

By 1784 there were approximately 250 Jewish families residing in Copenhagen (1200 persons). Of these, 70 families were so poor that they needed financial assistance. One hundred families were considered middle class and the rest economically comfortable. The poor Jews earned their meager income by peddling. They travelled throughout the country, visiting various villages and manors. This type of business enterprise had previously been prohibited following many complaints to the government. The Jews, however, could not engage in any other activity unless they received special royal permission. They were excluded from all guilds. Their children could not attend any public or private school, or be matriculated at the university.

The University of Copenhagen was at that time the only university in Denmark. In 1758, a Jew, S. J. Wolff was admitted to the university's medical school. By 1761 he had passed all his examinations, but the faculty still refused to grant any Jew a doctoral degree. The opposition was based upon the university's constitution, paragraph 51, which prohibited anyone: "who is known to possess false knowledge. . .to receive *Gradum Doctoris*." In 1770, professor J. C. Kåll of the Oriental Languages department posed a rhetorical question: "Does the conscience of a Christian permit him when he becomes sick, to engage a Jewish physician?" He quoted the church father, John Krysostomos (d.407), who considered it indecent and unbecoming for a Christian to seek any type of help from the devil, masters of magic or Jews. This prohibition had been reaffirmed by the church numerous times. He hoped, nevertheless, "that in the future, all, regardless of religious beliefs can receive a doctoral degree," concluding: "Why not, we live in Denmark!"

The university received a new constitution on May 7, 1788, wherein paragraph 51 was eliminated. Thus, the Jews were able to obtain the doctoral degree in all subjects, except theology. The first Jew awarded a doctoral degree was one deMeza. Barely had he received this honor, when he had himself baptized.

Restrictive forces were also present in the Jewish community, which was guided not only in the synagogue but in all communal matters by older members. This was done – in the opinion of the younger people – in a most dictatorial way.

Various liberal movements from the world at large made themselves felt among the Jews. A confrontation had to occur, and it began in 1787. A minor community struggle provided the spark. The opposing parties appealed to the government. The Jews actually asked the civil authorities to act as judges in the internal squabble. Thus, the first step was taken that eventually would lead to the emancipation of Danish Jewry.

The thirty years before the royal decree of March 29, 1814 was issued can be divided into three periods. Each period had its own leaders and spokesmen, each brought new challenges and problems. The conflicts and solutions which were arrived at formed the foundation for the Jews' acceptance into Danish society.

1787 – 1796

The first period was characterized by a confrontation between the "older" and more modern elements of the Jewish community and involved a religious question. As a rule, every week, some Polish Jews traveled to Copenhagen. At holiday time their numbers increased. It was considered a religious obligation to provide food and lodging for these travelers. The older element made arrangements that each visitor to the city was properly cared for according to Jewish tradition. Each individual received a food ticket for a Friday evening meal and a Saturday noon meal. The person whose name was written on the ticket had to provide the food. If he refused to serve the Polish Jews, who were considered "outlandish," he would be fined one crown per meal. This arrangement caused great dissatisfaction. Complaints were first directed to the leaders of the community, but they refused to change the arrangement. Thereupon, complaints were registered with the municipality of Copenhagen that the older element had misused its power, which, of course, the latter vehemently denied. In order to suppress the opposition, the older element invoked a ban of March 6, 1722. When one of the opposition came to the synagogue the following Sabbath in a wig not acceptable to older members, they would not mention his name in a *Me Sh'berach* prayer. Furthermore, he was not allowed to be called to the Torah. A fight broke out and caused a great scandal. Moses Fürst,[6] a leader of the opposition, subpoenaed members of the older elements to appear in court and defend themselves. They, in turn, appealed directly to the king to have the entire case dismissed by the judges. The Danish court ruled that the leaders of the Jewish community had the right to decide in internal matters.[7]

Another complaint to the government by the opposition was that the older element had mismanaged the financial records of the community. If a member did not pay a fine levied against him by the community officer, his name would be placed on a list. Upon his death, this list would be presented to his heirs, and if the fine was then not paid, he could not be buried in the Jewish cemetery.

The more serious complaint involved the probation of last wills and testaments and their administration. According to long established privileges, these matters were solely in the hands of the older element and the rabbi, and records were kept in Hebrew.

In a decree of December 7, 1757 the government had proclaimed that the Jews could probate their own wills, except in certain cases. If the heirs insisted, a Jewish will would be probated in open civil court. In 1786 a particular complaint respecting minors' rights of inheritance circulated within the Jewish community. A commission was established to investigate the matter. On July 24, 1789, a verdict was issued which stated, that if a majority of Jews wished to have a will involving minors probated in open court, it should be so done, but with the stipulation that the minors' money had to be deposited with the Public Trustee's Office.

---

[6] Moses Fürst 1784 – 1846, was the brother-in-law of Moses Mendelssohn, spiritual leader of the German Jewish reform movement.
[7] Julius Salomon og Josef Fischer, *Mindeskrift i Anledning af Hundredaarsdagen for Anordiningen af 29 Marts 1814* (København: J. Jørgensen & Co. 1914) p.39.

The next few years were relatively quiet. Led by Moses Fürst and Lazarus Wallach, the opposition still sought to break the older element's might and ruling power. It submitted various complaints to the chancellery regarding alleged financial irregularities in the community account. After a while the ruling group realized that a compromise had to be effected. Secret negotiations took place between the feuding parties. The result was the Compromise of March 10, 1791. It stipulated that four men should be elected to audit the community books, two from the older element and two from the opposition. One of the first provisions of the compromise was the abolition of meal tickets and fines for not serving the visiting foreign Jews. The agreement also provided for new taxes to be levied by majority vote and for an institution to be created to attend to orphans. Joel Wessely and Nathan Levin Meyer were chosen by the opposition to meet with their counterparts of the older element to audit the books. However, after one meeting took place, Wessely and Meyer complained, and the chancellery decided in their favor. It held that they had the right to investigate all books of the community, and that two officers of the community could then be present.

By 1796 various recommendations had been put forward to better the conditions of the Jewish community, including an "anonymous" one intended to be a blueprint for a constitution of the Danish Jewish community. It had been drafted by Gottlieb Euchel.[8] Euchel's interests were primarily to establish schools to enlighten the foreign-born and to abolish rabbinic jurisdiction. Being young (27 years) and influenced by the German Jewish reform movement, he was rather strong minded in his opinions. "Of all the Jewish people that I have met," he wrote, "the Jews of Copenhagen surpass others in immorality, prejudice, and superstition. True, I have met a handful of good and enlightened people among them. But what can they do to better the condition of the many? Will a few drops of fresh water make the oceans suitable for drinking?"

The time seemed ripe for a thorough revision of the basic laws governing the status of the Jews in Denmark. If Jews were to be ac-

---

[8] Born in Copenhagen 1767, Euchel studied in Berlin and Koenigsberg before establishing himself as a merchant in Copenhagen.

cepted into society at large, they had to submit unconditionally to the laws of the land. They could not have any special "rabbinic" laws.

Consequently, a royal commission was appointed to consider the prevailing conditions of the Jews as citizens of the country and to review their rights and obligations. In its report, issued on August 1, 1796, major sections dealt with the "laws as interpreted by their rabbis." The judges of Denmark do not know these laws, the commission stated. With the exception of public formalities, it is the rabbis who really decide all matters. However, the rabbis are not public officials. Their qualifications are not tested. In most cases, their rulings are based upon private opinion. In those cases where the rabbis take into consideration the law of the land (*Dine d'malchusa*),[9] the people are often ignorant of that law. Therefore its use is arbitrary and capricious.

The preamble to the report proclaimed that "Jews are obligated to conduct themselves according to Danish law. In no case can they invoke their own laws, or receive judgment according to these. The only exceptions from Danish law are those dealing with Christian religious services." The report then, in Chapter 1, launched into a consideration of laws pertaining to engagement, marriage, marriage-contracts, last wills and testaments. It concluded that all communal records and books as well as all public documents issued by the Jewish community should be written in the Danish or German language.

Other chapters of the report dealt with administration of the community, paid functionaries, and the election of officers. The report for the first time recommended that the rabbi, besides having a thorough knowledge of the Talmud, also possess a secular education and be well versed in the Danish and German languages. The official recorder of the community should also be able to read and write these languages, and be in charge of all official records and financial books. The report proposed the abolishment of taxes on kosher meat, establishment of a fund for the poor and needy (com-

---

[9] Shulchan Aruch, (Codes) Choshen Mishpot, No. 369 (Amsterdam: Emanuel ben Josef Atiah, 1669), p.391.

plete elimination of meal tickets), probate courts, and burial requirements. With respect to the latter, it held that no corpse should be buried before three days had passed after the demise.

The report, which had been worked out with the assistance of some Jews, was accepted by all members of the commission except Jeremias Henriques, who had replaced Wessely when he had died on March 25, 1794. One of five sons born to Abraham Moses Henriques of Nakskov, Henriques would only affirm the preamble, with its implication that Jews were to be considered on an equal basis with the rest of Danish society.

The Jewish community's response to the report was negative. Protests arose almost immediately. On Feb. 1, 1797, a written demurral was issued; it had been signed by all the representatives of the community, including D. A. Meyer and 167 heads of households. The document declared that the Christian members of the commission had expressed opinions on Jewish matters about which they had very little knowledge. Further, representatives of the community had communicated with the Jewish communities in Berlin and Altona regarding matters dealt with in the report. The responses received on November 5th and December 13th, 1796, clearly indicated that many of the ideas expressed by the commission were unacceptable to the Jewish faith.[10]

The Danish government moved gingerly in its implementation of the report. Only two important changes followed, both in the realm of social reform. The first was in regard to acceptance of Jewish boys into the various guilds. Until now the guilds had been closed to Jews. A special committee was appointed to oversee the absorption of the new apprentices, with twenty-eight masters agreeing to take them on. The government showed great interest in this matter and watched with care the development of these relationships. The annual *Kollegialtidende* of 1799 contains a list on which 44 Jews are classified in various guilds. Seven are masters: four calico-printing manufacturers, one die maker, one book printer and one artisan. Furthermore, seven are journeymen: three goldsmiths, two watchmakers, one saddler, two masons and three calico-printers. Finally,

---

[10] Salomon og Fisher, p. 49.

there are twenty-three apprentices: seven jewelers, four watchmakers, two calico-printers, four cabinet makers, one book binder, one die maker and two wool diers. In later editions the number of Jews in the various guilds increases moderately, and the guilds themselves vary considerably.

The second reform of this period – which in the beginning had very little effect – was in the field of education. A school was established in 1790. Its primary purpose was to teach poor Jewish children the three r's. The government followed this development also with great interest. The *Kollegialtidende* of 1798 states that the school had forty students, but thereafter the number decreased continuously. Only during the next period, when additional social reforms were made, did the education of poor Jewish students have the right impetus.

1797 – 1804

The next eight years were somewhat more relaxed. A fire in 1795 consumed the synagogue, the place where most of the Jewish community gathered. Thereafter, religious services were conducted in some dozen private homes. Each of these *shtibls* had its own set of religious officers. The economic crisis of 1799 did not make this situation any more pleasant.

Some of the small houses of worship had a spiritual leader, and they sought to guide the community in religious matters. Rabbi Hirsch Levy had served in this capacity as chief rabbi from 1741 – 1775, and had been succeeded by Rabbi Gedalia Levin, who died in 1793. Both rabbis were buried in the cemetery in Møllegade. Abraham Gedalia succeeded Levin as chief rabbi, but he was not an effective leader, and for all intents and purposes the internal affairs of the Jewish community in these years fell under the guidance of David Amsel Meyer. Born in 1753, Meyer obtained royal permission to start his own business at a very young age. Soon he was the first Jew to obtain the coveted wholesaler's license. In 1787 he became treasurer of the community and by 1791 its president. His great wealth made him the most influential member of the community with the power to maintain the status quo within the administration of the community.

The community had lost its center in the aforementioned fire. It was not long before a group was formed whose main object was to rebuild the synagogue. In 1799 a parcel of property was purchased in Krystalgade—the same property on which the synagogue is still located this day. However, before it could be started a controversy erupted. Those members of the community who had previously had a permanent seat in the "old" synagogue insisted on their right to the same seat in the "new" synagogue. Did they have such a right? Could they require compensation if the administration refused to give in to their demand? Unfortunately, the controversy took on such dimension that it had to be referred to the chancellery. The result was that the king, on September 3, 1803, established a new commission to investigate the entire matter of the rebuilding of the synagogue.

But now matters came to a halt, primarity because A. D. Meyer felt that the community was not united enough to bring this monumental undertaking forward. The revered chief rabbi, Abraham Gedalia, who served the congregation from 1793 - 1827, was not strong enough to head the project; nor was he able to bring all the feuding parties together. As time passed, members of the commission lost interest. A newly appointed board of representatives of the community had no greater success. Disunity among the members caused great friction. Some of the older members died. Others quit the body. By 1799 only three members were left.

Complaints to the chancellery began again, especially during the years 1800 - 1805. Primarily these were in regard to the financial records of the probate proceedings, welfare fund and the Jewish children's school.

Still, the Jewish population continued to grow. A census of the Jewish community on November 1, 1798, showed that there were 699 Jewish men and 792 Jewish women—1,491 Jews in a total population of 83,063 living in Copenhagen.

And there was progress of other kinds. In 1799 permission was granted to B. Koppel for his son, Nathan Bendix, ten years of age, to attend the Latin school in Nyborg without the requirement that he be baptized.

A special royal rescript of April 3, 1802, permitted Jews born in Denmark or being in possession of a royal certificate of safe conduct to deal in real estate.

But the most important developments were in regard to education. The children of wealthier Jews now gained admission to various private schools. Provision for the education of the less well-to-do was also not long in coming. In 1803, two members of the community, Hyman Jacob Bing and Levin Isaac Kalish, who had emigrated from Amsterdam to Copenhagen, established a school for Jewish students to which these youngsters might go. The subjects taught were the same as those taught in other public schools. And the school thrived. In a letter dated Copenhagen, June 10, 1813, and written on the occasion of the tenth anniversary of the school, Bishop Nikolai Edinger Balle praised the institution and its leaders.[11]

> I have been present at the public examinations. . . .I have noted with great satisfaction the love for our beloved king and fatherland which is taught there. Among the teachers as well as the students, motivation and interest can be noted. The teachers fulfill their sacred obligation with devotion and dedication.

An elementary school for the poor Jewish child, however, had still to be established.

As already mentioned, in 1799 Denmark experienced a short but acute economic crisis. This had its effect upon the business of A. D. Meyer. In the fall of 1799 Meyer traveled to Hamburg and Amsterdam to reestablish business connections. The following year he journeyed to Frankfurt on the Main. These trips had a signal effect upon Meyer. He met new people. He encountered new ideas. He saw the great potentialities that the new age of enlightenment pos-

---

[11] Bishop Balle is remembered as a friend of the Jews. After the great fire in 1795 he found an elderly Jew lying in the gutter, helpless and without a home. The bishop had the Jew brought to his palace and attended to all his needs. When the old man, shortly before his death a few weeks later, told the bishop he was worried that the usual Jewish funeral services would not be carried out, the bishop reassured him. After the Jew's death, Jewish religious services were conducted for seven days, mornings and evenings, in the bishop's palace.

sessed. Above all, he realized that he had been missing something unique, living outside the main sphere of the enlightenment. When he returned to Copenhagen, he seemed a changed man. He became more tolerant towards the younger element of the Copenhagen Jewish community. And though the latter had no great love for him, it would not undertake anything that went against his convictions. Thus, Meyer's leadership extended into the third period.

The real leader of this epoch, however, would not be Meyer, but his nephew, Mendel Levin Nathanson. Born in Altona on November 20, 1780, Nathanson came to Copenhagen after his Bar Mitzvah without being able to speak one word of Danish. His secular education was very sparse. At 18 years of age he went on a short trip to England to learn firsthand the trade of a large country. He returned to Copenhagen after a year, married and started his own business.

His first work for the Jewish community was in 1803. Poverty and destitution was great among the majority of Copenhagen's Jews. He established a flour and bread fund in order to provide these basic items to the poor at a low price. Young and relatively unknown either within or outside the community, he puzzled his fellow Jews in Copenhagen, who simply could not understand him. But Nathanson had still greater ambitions. And he possessed the ability to challenge the imagination of the most influential people. He was also fortunate in the two men who became his associates, Gottlieb Euchel and Dr. Samuel Jacobi. Euchel, mentioned previously, had participated as a young man in the discussion regarding the report of 1796. Jacobi, born in Poland, had studied medicine at various German universities, and was now a physician in Copenhagen. Vice-president of the royal medical society, Jacobi was also a member of the community's board of representatives.

Together with these two men, Nathanson began planning a free school for all Jewish boys. In this endeavor he won the backing of old D. A. Meyer. A committee was formed. The plans were endorsed by the most influential members of the Jewish community. Thus Nathanson's most important work was launched as the second period drew to a close. The dawn of the third period, unfortunately, was not bright.

1805 – 1814

The period sometimes called the Nathanson Reform Period, begins amid a series of national catastrophes. The British attack on Denmark in 1807. The bombing of Copenhagen. Seven years of devastating war. National bankruptcy. The treaty at Kiel. The loss of Norway. But despite all these disasters, young (24 years) Nathanson did not give up his hope to further the emancipation of Denmark's Jews. And his program went forward. In 1805 the Free Boys School was founded. In 1806 the special tax on kosher meat was abolished. The same year an income tax was levied on all members of the Jewish community according to their earnings. In 1808, Nathanson was chosen spokesman of a committee to congratulate King Frederick VI on his coronation. In the same year, Jews were permitted to join the armed forces. In 1809 the old board of representatives resigned, and a new board, geared to reconstruction, was appointed by the chancellery. In 1810, official government records for the Jews were established and a Jewish school for girls, *Carolineskolen*, was opened. In 1811, a new Jewish burial society was founded. The following year, Nathanson was instrumental in obtaining a new text book, in Danish, for the Jewish schools. In 1813, the word ''Jew' was officially abolished as descriptive of an individual in a profession or occupation. Finally, in March, 1814, The Royal Decree of 1814 was promulgated, declaring Jews to be full and equal citizens of Denmark.

Not all of this progress came easily. The Free Boys School started amidst great difficulties. Nathanson personally approached members of the community to enroll their sons in the institution. He also obtained funds for its support from one hundred and twenty-five families. During the bombing of Copenhagen in 1807, the school burned down. The project had to be started all over again. The first administration of the school consisted of Nathanson, Euchel and Jacobi. The first class had 55 students, an acceptable number for those times. The principal, Gedalia Moses, had been brought in from Stockholm, Sweden. Although he was not able to speak one word of Danish, he proved to be a good choice. He soon became proficient in the language, and knew how to gain the respect and love of his students. The boys were not only taught the regular academic subjects, but provided also with suitable occupations once they left the institution. Nathanson looked after their physical needs as well, personally, insuring that they all had enough food, clothing and shoes. He wanted each boy to be properly prepared when he entered a guild or merchant house. He invested his personal fortune to further all these matters.

Nathanson's opposition to the tax on kosher meat stemmed from his observation that it involved a monopoly, and that the tax was most unfair and oppressive to the poor. Furthermore, those Jewish families which did not buy kosher meat were exempt from the tax. Nathanson thought the entire arrangement intolerable. Consequently, he asked the chancellery to abolish this ancient and inequitable levy and in its stead institute a tax on the personal income of all members of the Jewish community. On August 15, 1806, a royal decree was issued, permitting Lion Israel, Moses Bendix, Gerson Melchior and Nathanson, with the consent of the community board of representatives, to assess and collect taxes of all the Jews residing in Copenhagen, with the exception of Jews on welfare. The decree in fact, made into law a proposal originally promulgated by the commission of 1796.

Nathanson's prominent position among his fellow Jews led to his being chosen spokesman for the committee to congratulate King Frederick VI on his coronation (1808). His words on that occasion reflected the sentiments of many Danish Jews. He spoke of ". . . the pain that we all have experienced by the loss of the most noble among kings, your highly regarded and saintly father, our king Christian VII," and expressed gratitude "for all the grace and kindness that has come our way. . .and the human conditions amongst our citizens. . . . Above all else, although we are not members of the State religion, we are called sons of the land. . .Danish citizens."

His speech concluded with the following words:

> Your royal majesties. . .our fathers saw the splendor of the Almighty on Mount Sinai. . . . Times go on and cities disappear. . .but the Almighty is One, and One is the Almighty. . . . He, the G-d of our fathers, G-d of all mankind,

who is called upon in temples, synagogues and churches, upon Him we call, that He may let His grace and mercy shine over your royal throne.

In 1809, after the old board of representatives had resigned, Nathanson and others petitioned the chancellery that a new board, consisting of seven members, be appointed. The request was granted. The opening words of the reply from the chancellery are most important, for they herald the royal decree of five years later: "Since the chancellery has for some time expressed to His majesty a desire for a better arrangement of the Jewish citizens in public matters, we hereby grant your request." It would seem that the attitude of the government towards the Jews was being examined in various departments, for the following year, on May 29, 1810 a royal decree was issued, obligating the Jewish community to keep books and records, verified by the government, in regard to births, deaths and marriages. The financial records and probate records were also scrutinized and brought in order. Since 1805 the probate records had been in Danish. From now on all official books of the community were to be in Danish.

The newly appointed seven-member board of representatives included M. Wessely, broker; Samuel Jacobi, physician; Joseph Raphael, dealer in dry goods; Falk Ahrensen, merchant; Josua Glückstadt, Gerson M. Melchior and Ruben Henriques, Jr. The first decision of the board in 1810 was to establish a school for girls. Two members of the board, Wessely and Raphael, together with Nathanson, prepared plans for the school. The board of representatives secured permission from the king to have as the school's patroness, Princess Caroline. Hence it was called *Carolineskolen*. The school opened with 52 students on October 28, 1809, the birthday of the princess. Most of the teachers were non-Jews. As at the Boys School, needy students annually received clothing and shoes. The financial needs of the institution were in the beginning underwritten by the community. Later it received the Meyer endowment of 30,000 Reichsthaler, which insured its future existence.

The next problem that Nathanson undertook involved the burial society. That body had been in existence for a long time, but it had not always done its work well. There was the matter of quick burials. In one case, a man had died on a Friday morning at 7 and was buried at 2 P.M. the same day, because the society did not want to let the corpse remain uninterred until after the Sabbath. Also the selection of graves had caused numerous frictions. Those who had been more "orthodox" were buried in different rows from those who had been less so, though in death all should be equal.

The custodian of the Jewish cemetery in Møllegade also kept a tavern, where people ate and drank, played cards and smoked while the corpse was being washed and prepared for burial. In 1807, British soldiers had been billeted with the custodian. They caused havoc with the graves and monuments. When some of their comrades died, they buried them in the cemetery. The graves remain there to this day.

All these things Nathanson wanted to change. Therefore he started the New Burial Society and gathered numerous members of the community to join him. But his uncle, old D. A. Meyer, who had been most helpful in other matters, was violently opposed to this reform. Nevertheless, Nathanson succeeded. The by-laws of the New Burial Society were confirmed by a decree of May 11, 1811. Furthermore, the chancellery issued a proclamation that no corpse could be buried unless 72 hours had passed since death. One of the first to be buried by the new society was Dr. Samuel Jacobi, Nathanson's early ally. While previously only Jews had attended Jewish funerals, on this occasion members of the government, military and clergy were present.

In 1812, Nathanson had a *Textbook for the Jewish Religion* translated into Danish from the German and submitted the book to the chancellery for approval. A commission consisting of Councillor Kall, Gedalia Moses (director of the Boys School), Gottlieb Euchel and government attorney Lassen, recommended approval of the book for use by Danish Jewish students. In the same year, the first old age home *Godgørenhed* (Beneficence) was established for 24 Jewish widows and poverty stricken families of the community.

As the appointment of the new board of representatives was only temporary, the chancellery undertook to make all necessary arrangements for a permanent board including provision for the election of the community officers. A final draft resolution on the matter, submitted in August, 1813, contained a short history of the Jews since their arrival in Denmark. An outline followed wherein various improvements in the social conditions of Jews were enumerated. Schools, admittance to the guilds, and other communal and religious institutions had all helped prepare the Jews to become useful citizens of the Danish state. With minor differences, the royal resolution of August 13, 1813, concurred with this draft resolution. The king wanted the final act to take effect in all of Denmark including Slesvig-Holstein, but due to "local conditions" the resolution could not be applied to these two duchies.

The draft resolution had contained the following proviso: "It would be advantageous to know the catechism of the Jewish religion. It would be advisable, both for the youth born in Denmark, as well as foreign Jews coming to Denmark, to declare in a proper manner their affiliation with the Jewish religion, before they would be considered real members of the community." On these grounds the draft resolution was returned to the chancellery for further study.

Two main problems remained. From a letter from Nathanson to A. S. Ørsted, a government official,[12] undated but most probably written in October, 1813, we find that Nathanson – not the board of representatives – negotiated with the chancellery. Nathanson wanted the board of representatives to be primarily tax assessors, a position with which Ørsted agreed. Furthermore, he won the principle that the community should elect the rabbi and the representatives, not the chancellery. Finally, Nathanson tried to negotiate the most sensitive point, the issue of the public oath. Ørsted was of the opinion that the wording of the oath should be changed. But he did not want to postpone the final decree any further. A special commission had to be established to deal exclusively with this thor-

---

[12] Anders Sandøe Ørsted, 1778 – 1860, wrote critical analyses of Danish and Norwegian laws; became a judge at 22 years of age; in 1813 left the Danish Supreme Court and joined the government; became prime minister of Denmark in 1842.

ny problem, since the wording of the oath also would apply to non-Jews. This matter was not solved until 1843.

On March 29, 1814, a new era dawned upon the Jews of Denmark. The royal decree was proclaimed, granting full citizenship to Denmark's Jews. The seeds had been planted for a successful modern democracy in which all might participate.

IV

The Royal Decree of 1814

The royal decree of March 29, 1814, which declared "what the followers of the Mosaic religion, who reside in the Kingdom of Denmark, have to observe," is so important a document in this history that it deserves to be included here in its entirety.

We, Frederick the Sixth
by the grace of G-d, King of Denmark, the Venders and Gothers, Duke of Slesvig, Holstein, Ditmarsken and Oldenburg, hereby proclaim: We have considered it beneficial to make the following proclamation in regard to the followers of the Mosaic religion who reside in Our kingdom of Denmark:

1.

Those of the followers of the Mosaic religion, who are born in Our kingdom of Denmark, or have received permission to settle therein, should be permitted to enjoy equality with the rest of the citizens to support themselves in every lawful way. They must follow the civil laws of the country, unless they have received special exemption from this decree. In no civil matter can they find refuge in the Jewish laws, or the so-called rabbinic regulations or customs. From this follows, that they must [abide] in all matters regarding probates, public welfare and education (except religious instruction) as well as any other matter, which is not an inseparable part of religion by the jurisdiction of the place and public authorities where they live. Exempt are those of the Mosaic religion who reside in our royal capital city of Copenhagen and [follow] the regulations stipulated dated this day today.

2.

Immediately following this proclamation, the police authorities, each in their district should obtain a census of all residents following the Mosaic religion. In this census everyone should be entered with a family name, which should be used unchanged by son after father. This census, which should be formulated in accordance with those tables attached to this decree, under Letr. A, should be submitted in Copenhagen directly by the chief of police, and in other places by the local authorities to Our Danish chancellery. Annually a census should be taken in the same manner, and submitted before the end of the month of January.

3.

All instruments of debts, last wills and testaments, marriage contracts and all other documents which are executed by the followers of the Mosaic religion, should, if they expect to have the validity of a document be written in the Danish or German language with gothic or latin letters. These said documents should use the calendar as is customary in Our kingdom. Similarly, all business records, which the followers of the Mosaic religion keep or have kept for them, should be written in the Danish or German language with gothic or latin letters, using the normal calendar as is customary in Our kingdom, if they are to be deemed valid.

If such a document or business record is issued or kept in another language or in another matter as prescribed herein, and a dispute arises in regard to these, the document or business record kept and written according to this decree is to be accepted.

4.

All official records of the community of the Mosaic religion – which will be ordered later – regarding information of the age of persons, marriages, deaths or other matters about which in civil matters can become questionable, should likewise be kept in the Danish or German language with gothic or latin letters according to the normal calendar customary in Our kingdom and Our lands. These official records should be authorized in Copenhagen by the municipality and outside [Copenhagen] by the county administration's officer, who should ascertain explicitly that these records are kept according to the prescribed manner. In a contrary case, the individual should be liable to prosecution.

5.

Members of the Mosaic religion who execute marriage contracts or last wills and testaments after Our decree has been promulgated, and which contain provisions which are outside or contrary to Danish laws, should not have any powers or obligation, unless they have received Our gracious confirmation. Those marriage contracts, and last wills and testaments which already have been executed, will, if they are submitted within one year to Our Danish chancellery – with exact and verbatim translation if they are not worded in the Danish language, and with an authenticated copy of the translation – receive Our gracious confirmation, if they do not vary from prevailing rules of such documents. Those [documents] which are not submitted within this time limit for confirmation, will, if they have no basis in the laws of the land, be considered invalid.

6.

Any marriage which is contrary to Danish law may not be solemnized between followers of the Mosaic religion, unless they have obtained Our special most highest permission.

7.

Divorce from table and bed among the followers of the Mosaic religion may not take place except by the authorities in accordance with the regulations of May 23, 1800, announced permission. No marriage may be annuled by judgment or through Our Danish chancellery except by Our most gracious announced permission.

8.

No representative, priest or any member of the Mosaic religion community may dare to obstruct or disturb anybody of the Mosaic religion's followers in the performance of lawful trade, under the pretense of religion, or assume any power over their domestic condition.

Consequently, the permission granted on March 6, 1722, to use the light ban, and which by this decree is made unnecessary, is hereby repealed completely.

9.

The followers of the Mosaic religion may not have a synagogue except where they have acquired or hereafter will acquire [a place] unless by Our most gracious permission.

10.

Every synagogue shall have a priest, who shall be authorized by Us, and who shall enjoy the income of the position, which We shall decide in more details. We shall, furthermore, authorize a chief priest who shall live in Copenhagen. All other community priests should be subordinate to him in all official matters.

11.

No priestly act may be performed by anyone, except of those priests authorized by Us. They are [our officials] and are responsible for their actions to Us. Those who already possess the right to perform priestly acts at such a community may continue to do so for three months after the promulgation of this decree. Thereafter, it shall be completely prohibited for them to commence such acts unless We will employ them at a synagogue. Upon application, and found worthy, [they may] expect this [employment].

12.

It is the obligation of the representatives or directors for the Mosaic religious communities, in those places where permission has been granted to have a synagogue, to keep records, or by men appointed by the local authority, to keep two identical journals where births, deaths and marriages are recorded with name and date, when the births, deaths or marriages took place. These records, which should be authorized in the manner as stated in paragraph 4, should be arranged according to this decree attached table Letr. B. Those that keep these [records] should frequently confer with each other. Both journals should not remain under the same roof for one night. Twice yearly, namely May 1 and November 1, these books should be presented to the authorities, who by their signature should attest that [the journals] correspond with each other.

In those places where there is no synagogue, the authority of the place should have a separately composed table, Letr. B, and records authorized by the authority, wherein all children who are born by the followers of the Mosaic religion, all deaths that may occur and all marriages that may be solemnized be recorded.

13.

In order to facilitate the above mentioned paragraphs, and that it can be observed explicitly, reports shall be rendered to him who keeps the records by parents regarding births, by surviving spouses regarding deaths, or by anyone who is closest and arranging these details in such events; in case of marriage, by the priest who has solemnized the wedding ceremony.

A fine of 20 to 5000 Rbdlr. will be levied, depending upon the offense or the circumstance of the guilty if the reporting is not done within twenty-four hours. If birth, death or wedding occurs in a place where there is no synagogue, and where the reporting has to be done by the local authority, the individual will be obligated, under equal penalty, to report with the first mail opportunity to the representatives of the community where the births, deaths and married belong. The representatives must immediately register [such events] in the church records of the congregation.

14.

Since We have authorized a textbook for religious [instruction] for the youth of the followers of the Mosaic religion, all boys and girls are hereafter obligated, at a public examination, to demonstrate that they have learned the teachings as outlined in the book. Thereafter they should ceremoniously take their religious vows and promise that, out of their own free will, they will not act against the fundamental rules as stated in this book.

15.

These public examinations may be conducted any place where We most graciously have given permission to have a synagogue. No other than the appointed priest or those men who have been authorized by Our Danish chancellery may conduct such examinations.

16.

No one may be permitted to take these examinations - which are given twice annually, namely the first week in May and the first week in November - unless he has reached his thirteenth birthday.

17.

Those who have already reached their fourteenth year, or have arrived in this country after they have reached this age, after the proclamation of this decree, will be exempt from taking this public test. Hereafter, no follower of the Mosaic religion may be sworn, enter into matrimony, be recorded as a journeyman in any guild, obtain citizenship in any town, engage in any type of business under whatever name, be registered in the roster of students, or [be considered] as of age to master his own possessions, unless they have submitted to the above mentioned test and rendered their oath of belief in the prescribed manner.

18.

The priest employed by the synagogue shall keep exact records of the youth who are preparing to give their religious vows. This record, which must be authorized and kept according to paragraph 4, should be arranged according to table attached to this decree, Letr, C.

19.

Any follower of the Mosaic religion, regardless if he belongs to the German or Portuguese congregation, wishing to stay longer in Our kingdom of Denmark – except for a transit journey, which can last no more than fourteen days – shall, disregarding sex or age, submit an application for a longer stay to our Danish chancellery. A fine of 50 to 1000 Rbdlr. can be levied according to the severity of the offense. Under certain circumstances We have empowered [the chancellery] to grant permission for residency of several months. Should the alien, during his permitted stay, engage in an unlawful business transaction, in the so-called "Skakkeri," begging or other unlawful matters, he should be charged and punished according to law. Immediately after having served his punishment, the police authority should expel [the alien] from the country.

20.

In those places, where the followers of the Mosaic religion have separate congregations, the representatives and directors are obligated, under penalty of fine, to report to the police the arrival of any alien to the congregation. In this way they should assist the police in supervising such aliens.

All persons concerned have most graciously to comply.
Given in Our royal city Copenhagen, the 29th of
    March 1814
                    Frederik R
Kaas   Cold   Bülow   Monrad   Ørsted   Berner   Lassen

The royal decree of March 29, 1814 was well received by the Jewish community. What the decree basically did was to ratify and confirm the position of Jews as it had evolved for a number of years.

How did the Jews of Denmark benefit by the decree? The first and most important gain is found in paragraph 1, which states that the Jews shall have the same civil rights as other citizens. They were entitled and permitted to support themselves in any lawful manner. The decree made it, however, explicitly clear that in regard to any civil ordinance a Jew could not take refuge in Jewish or rabbinic laws. An additional point was the provision pertaining to probate. Henceforth, all probate cases were to be decided by the special probate courts under the jurisdiction of the royal court. The Jews had to keep their business records and other public documents in the Danish or German languages. The documents had previously been kept in Hebrew. The Portuguese and German Jews were to be considered as one entity in regard to election of members to the community's board of representatives.

The decree further stated that an annual census be taken of all members of the Jewish community. The board of representatives was to be elected by the members of the community and not, as previously, appointed by the chancellery. Finally, religious examination of the Jewish youth was introduced. The text used for this test was based upon the previously mentioned textbook on the Jewish religion.[1]

---

[1] Julius Salomon og Josef Fischer, *Mindeskrift i Anledning af Hundredaarsdagen for Anordningen af 29 Marts 1814* (København: J, Jørgensen & Co. 1914), p. 72.

Additional books – in Hebrew and Danish – began to appear after 1814. On July 7, 1785, the Jew, Israel Moses Israel, received permission to establish a printing press for the Hebrew, Chaldean, Aramaic and other Oriental languages.[2] Among the books printed in Danish and Hebrew in Copenhagen were *Book of Devotion for Jews* by A. Gottlob, 1843, and *Collection of Prayers* by M. Wahrman, 1848. The latter was to be used for first instruction in Hebrew.[3]

The basic thought underlying the decree was that Danish Jews should enjoy all rights granted to all other citizens. Nothing was to be done to curtail these rights or hamper the Jews' free exercise of them. But the Jewish community had, of course, to pay a price for its newly won position.

For the first time, the civil government would have a voice in the internal administration of the community. Such "foreign" control had previously been deemed totally unacceptable. The most important provision in this respect was that Danish law regarding marriages also applied to the Jews. This meant that interfaith marriages had to be fully recognized by the Jewish community. Moreover, rabbinic letter of divorce (*Get*) had in the future no legal standing.

The community acceded to official supervision in regard to the maintenance of the synagogue and the wages paid to religious functionaries. The community, furthermore, accepted and tolerated official clearance of religious textbooks. Above all else, the youth of the Jewish community, upon reaching the age of 14 years, submitted to a religious test. Such an examination had actually no basis in Jewish law. The test which soon became known as "confirmation," was a ceremony which introduced Jewish youth into Danish society at large. Held semi-annually, it was intended to confirm that boys and girls, between the ages of 14 and 16, were properly instructed in national history, ethics and general Jewish concepts. Bar Mitzvah, in the eyes of the government, was a concern of the internal Jewish community only, and only confirmed that a young man

---

[2] An early Hebrew book, printed in Copenhagen, was *N'teay Shashuim* a collection of Hebrew poems by Nathan Kalkar, 1834.

[3] Julius Margolinsky, Chief librarian, Jewish Community Library, Copenhagen.

had reached his thirteenth birthday. Although, nowadays "confirmation" is no longer mandatory, the examination is still given; it is mostly taken by girls.

Strangely enough, it was Nathanson who had wanted the government to appoint the community representatives. Ørsted, however, felt that a more democratic approach would be advantageous and that the community at large should elect them. This arrangement was actually first achieved by a special rescript of February 18, 1848, which instituted community elections without further approval of the Danish government.

In this rescript, Nathanson was able to get the title "rabbi" substituted for "priest," and "synagogue" for "church." The original language had been based on the notion that all "rabbinic" expressions regarding laws, functions, houses of worship were unacceptable to the government. But common sense—as well as strict meaning—soon brought the words rabbi, synagogue, chief rabbi into regular usage.

With equal rights granted to all Jews, the old distinctions between Ashkenazim and Sephardim gradually disappeared.

One may well wonder what was not achieved by the decree? The Jewish community soon discovered that there were five areas in which the document was unsatisfactory. The first of these was maintenance of the restriction on foreign Jews traveling in Denmark. These Jews had to obtain a "letter of safe conduct"; even for short visits to the country, they needed special permission. They also had to designate their place of residence for the duration of the stay. The Jews of Copenhagen, nevertheless, did not see anything wrong with this stipulation of the law. In fact, as late as 1840, a group of Copenhagen Jews asked the chancellery to impose stronger restrictions on immigrants. The request, however, was turned down.

The second area was the requirement that the Jewish community maintain its own welfare fund. When the general welfare system of Copenhagen was reorganized in 1799, all other religious welfare funds – namely, those of the Lutheran, Reformed and Catholic communities—were combined and united. The government, at that time, did not consider the Jews as an established entity in the city. Since Jews continued to administer their own welfare fund until after 1848, we may assume that some Jews wanted it so. There were many needy Jews in Copenhagen, and the Jewish welfare system was more effective than that administered by the government. Still, Jews were excluded from a governmental service by virtue of the arrangement.

The third area concerned the oath. The oath – *More Judaico* as it was known – still contained the despicable wording promulgated by the law of September 15, 1747. In 1815, the chancellery asked the theological faculty of Copenhagen University to recommend a new oath. The faculty, however, demurred, advising the chancellery not to alter the formula by which Jews swore allegiance to the king. Not until 1843 was it changed.

The fourth area was the law respecting marriages, which stated that only those marriages which were permitted according to Danish law could be solemnized.

The fifth area, perhaps the most painful of all, was that of public employment. While the letter of the law qualified Jews for all public offices, too many loopholes were still left after the decree for prejudiced bureaucrats to exclude them.

The Jewish community, nevertheless, looked upon the royal decree of 1814 as a divine blessing. It expressed its appreciation in various ways. Many bequests were made in honor of the decree. When old D. A. Meyer died in 1822, he left behind such a bequest involving a great amount of money. Through Nathanson's intervention, not only did Jews receive benefits from this fortune, but also non-Jewish institutions which fostered the arts and sciences. It is estimated that in the first thirty years after the decree was proclaimed a total of more than 200,000 Reichsthaler were bequeathed to the Jewish community in its name. Appropriate arrangements were made to commemorate the decree of March 29, 1814 on special occasions. For example, scholarly works were issued on its 100th anniversary, as well as on its 150th anniversary, the former edited by Julius Salomon and Josef Fischer, the latter by Julius Margolinsky and Poul Meyer.

Nathanson, who had been so successful in furthering the emancipation of Danish Jewry, joined the board of representatives in 1816. Within this board, he felt he could achieve a reformation of the religious services in the synagogue which he believed necessary. He was now so powerful that no member of the board would vote against him. And he was convinced that he had the right person to create the changes he desired.

The law of 1814 had authorized the establishment of a new religious office ("Kateket") within the community. The kateket had as his main function to teach religion and prepare and conduct the required religious tests. In Copenhagen he had to give instruction in religion in the two free schools. Outside Copenhagen, kateket were employed by the Jewish communities in Odense and Fredericia. In these cities additional functions, such as weddings, were performed by these religious functionaries.

As the old chief rabbi, Abraham Gedalia, could not be relied upon to perform the requirements of the newly passed law, a young man, Isaak Noah Mannheimer was appointed by royal decree on July 17, 1816, to be the kateket. Nathanson was convinced that Mannheimer was the man to push through his reforms.

The first Jewish "confirmation service" was conducted by Mannheimer on May 19, 1817. Prime minister Kaas, other public officials as well as priests were among the great assembly. A Danish priest's translation of the 33rd Psalm, was chanted to organ music as the service opened. Then other Danish songs were sung. A lecture was delivered in Danish. The *konfirmanter* were publicly tested, and at the conclusion of the service, another psalm, also in Danish, was recited.

Thereafter, Mannheimer instituted Wednesday evening "devotional exercises," during which all prayers were recited in Danish. Hostility to these changes soon arose. A strong and vocal opposition to the kateket's reformist tendencies was launched under the guidance of prominent members of the community. Three former members of the board of representatives were counted among the opposition: Salomon Seligman Trier, Ruben Henriques, Jr., and Gerson Moses Melchior. Nathanson's own brother, Joel Levin Nathanson, also protested sharply against what Mannheimer was doing. The feuding became so intense that in 1823 Mannheimer left Copenhagen for Vienna. There were rumors that Nathanson also intended to leave Copenhagen for Wandsbeck, Germany, but these proved to be unfounded. In the end, Nathanson was forced to acknowledge that, although the government was well disposed towards the Jews, the community at large was not yet ready for reform.

The difficulties of Jews in attaining public office, nevertheless continued. Some Jews thought that only baptism would open the doors closed against them and converted to Christianity. Others had their children baptized but remained within the community. Persons bearing such well-known names as Nathanson (Nansen), Herforth, David, Hertz, Henriques, Warburg, Kalkar, Delbanco, Jacobi became Christians. The children of some even became pastors in the established Danish church.

On November 8, 1827, old chief rabbi Gedalia died after serving the community for thirty-six eventful years. The following year, Abraham Alexander Wulff was appointed chief rabbi. Wulff had previously served the Jewish community in Upper Hesse. More conservative than Mannheimer, he nevertheless possessed an academic education. He soon received a royal appointment and was given detailed instruction regarding the dress he should wear at religious services.

Wulff's first task was to organize the construction of the new synagogue in Krystalgade. He was able to achieve enough unity among the various feuding parties to raise 27,000 Reichsthaler in voluntary contributions for this purpose. A mortgage of approximately 70,000 Reichsthaler was granted by the government, and the plans of the architect, Professor Hetsch, were approved. Progress now was swift. The cornerstone was laid in 1830, and on April 12, 1833, the synagogue was dedicated.

Chief Rabbi Wulff submitted an "agenda" for religious services to the chancellery for consideration and approval. The "agenda," which was approved, called for all prayers to be recited in Hebrew. Special prayers (*P'yutim*) were eliminated. As the services evolved, the weekly sermon was in the beginning delivered in German, later in Danish. A special prayer for king and country and the benediction and blessing, (in which the rabbi raised his hands as had the *kohanim* of old) were recited in Danish. The numerous mourners' *kaddishim* were eliminated. Only one *Me Sh'berach* prayer was recited on Sabbath morning after seven men had been called to the Torah. No monetary donations were publicly announced. Holiday prayers and services followed the traditional order. On Rosh Hashono and Yom Kippur many prayers of supplication (*S'lichos*), in addition to the *P'yutim*, were left out.

As Wulff began to institute the new service, a new battle began taking shape. Rumors began to fly that the new synagogue would become a model of the Reform temple in Hamburg, and that Wulff, who had come from Germany, would gradually introduce the Reform service of that city. Thus Moses Levy began his life-long battle against the chief rabbi.

Moses Levy was born in Copenhagen in 1795. His father, Hyman Hertz Levy, also called Chayim Kook, had received a letter of safe conduct in 1790. He had come from Amsterdam, married Pouline Meyer, a daughter of Meyer Isaac, whose father, Isaak Jacob, had settled in Copenhagen in 1735.

On June 1, 1832 King Frederick VI received a letter from Moses Levy and his brother Heiman Levy, wherein they respectfully petitioned the king not to permit any type of choir singing in the newly built synagogue or any elimination, shortening or changing of prayers. (See Appendix II.) The brothers also asked the king not to allow any language other than Hebrew to be used in prayers or any new prayers to be introduced. The letter was turned over to the chancellery, which in turn asked chief rabbi Wulff for an opinion in the matter. When Wulff spurned the petition, Moses Levy fired off another, requesting permission to open a private synagogue in his own house in Laederstraede. His request was denied. Levy, nevertheless, opened the synagogue in his home, and it became a permanent institution in Copenhagen. Twice daily religious services were conducted there, until 1957, when this private synagogue was closed.

Moses Levy had two daughters. One died in childhood. When the other reached the age of "confirmation," Levy would not allow her to be examined by Wulff. Instead, he had her take a written test administered by a Christian priest. The latter had assured him that this was acceptable according to law. Nevertheless, Wulff requested numerous times that Levy send his daughter to him to be confirmed. Each time Levy refused. When the chancellery commanded Levy that he submit his daughter to Wulff's examination, Levy appealed the order and was rejected. In the meantime, the daughter had become engaged to be married. Confirmation had to take place before the wedding. Levy asked the kateket, Levison, to conduct the test, but Levison refused. Finally Levy had to give in. But he revenged himself by submitting his daughter's official wedding license barely two hours before the ceremony. This happened in 1849.

Levy, assisted by his new son-in-law and other followers, attacked Wulff on numerous occasions. In essence, Levy's group wanted to maintain religious services as they had been conducted for hundreds of years.

While these controversies kept the rabbi and community occupied, new ideas were fermenting in Denmark. Clouds of war gathered again above the horizon of Slesvig-Holstein. The spirit of tolerance, understanding and equal rights, blazing through Europe, ultimately reached Denmark. Thus, as the chancellery, parliament and king prepared for battle with the Prussian-Austrian army from the south, they realized that the cooperation of the entire country would be needed. In the prevailing spirit of liberty, the country's political leaders drafted, voted, and proclaimed the new Constitution of June 5, 1849, which gave complete freedom to all citizens of Denmark, including the Jews.

V

The Jewish Community and Its Institutions

Most of the Jewish institutions in Copenhagen had a long and proud history. They had been established at various times as need arose, been maintained for decades in dignity and love, and been cherished by all for the traditions and customs which they honored.

Any Jewish community had – from time immemorial – a synagogue, a school and a cemetery. Jews in Denmark, from their earliest settlement, had maintained these three basic institutions in order to be considered a *K'hilla*.

Copenhagen's main synagogue, located in Krystalgade, designed by Professor Hetsch of the Royal Academy for Fine Arts, had been built between 1825 – 1833, and dedicated on April 12, 1833.[1] Prior to this, a number of other synagogues had existed in Copenhagen but these were either destroyed by the fires which swept the city at the end of the 18th century or were closed when the beautiful, imposing structure in Krystalgade was opened.

Except one: the synagogue in Laederstraede – the old Jewish neighborhood in Copenhagen – founded by Moses Levy Kook. This small house of worship, maintained and administered by Moses Levy's descendants for more than a century, is now protected by the Danish Government's Interior Department.

---

[1] Max Friediger, *Jødernes Historie* (Copenhagen: P. Haase & Søns Forlag, 1934), p.350.

When, after World War II, the Jews returned from Sweden in May, 1945, religious services could not be conducted in the main synagogue in Krystalgade. The official Danish community therefore decided to hold its services in the Laederstraede synagogue. A full report with pictures of this religious event appeared in the newspaper *Billed Bladet*, in June of that year.

In later years other synagogues would be established. The most important of these was the *Machazekay Hadass*, founded in 1910 by the supporters of Dr. Lewenstein at the time of his conflict with the Jewish community of Copenhagen. Dr. Lewenstein, having a life contract, insisted he would only officiate at religious ceremonies conducted according to Orthodox Jewish tradition. The community demanded that he conduct all previously performed rites. When Lewenstein refused, the question of breach of contract was brought to court. Eventually, the Danish Supreme Court decided in favor of Dr. Lewenstein. Afterwards Lewenstein accepted a call to Zurich, Switzerland, where he ministered for more than forty years.

The *Machazekay Hadass* was originally located in Aabenraa, the old neighborhood where most of the refugees from Eastern European pogroms lived, but in 1934 it was moved to larger and more modern quarters in Ole Suhrsgade. Members of the *Machazekay Hadass* employed their own rabbi, had their own shochet, maintained their own Hebrew school, and tried not to partake of the other religious facilities provided by the main synagogue in Krystalgade.

Still there were some facilities they could not avoid, such as the *mikvah* and the cemetery. Moreover, birth and death certificates could only be issued by the office of the chief rabbi. Only he could perform marriage ceremonies which were valid in the eyes of the Danish state. Various methods were improvised to reduce contact with the main synagogue and its functions. People would travel to Germany to get married. Parents would "import" a mohel from Germany for a newborn son. The *Machazekay Hadass* never had its own *mikvah* or cemetery, but always used those of Krystalgade. In this connection, it should be stated that there was no Conservative or Reform congregation in Denmark.

The main synagogue in Krystalgade was financially maintained by annual taxes collected by the government from every Jew belonging to the Jewish community. Other places of worship for Jews were supported exclusively by voluntary contributions.

In addition to the *Machazekay Hadass*, two small prayer rooms were founded in Copenhagen in later years. One was in the home of Julius Ruben, who together with his six sons and grandsons maintained a *minyon* in Tordenskjoldsgade. Ruben conducted services on Sabbath and holidays; very few outsiders ever attended these. Ruben's prayer room ceased to exist before 1940, when Julius Ruben passed away.

The second prayer room was located in Kronprinsessegade. Its interior was much like a synagogue, with permanent pews and a special place for women. It belonged to George and Naphtali Cohn, prominent Danish Jews. George Cohn was an ambassador and special advisor on international law to the Danish foreign ministry. Naphtali was a judge on international tribunals and a counselor at the Supreme Court of Denmark. This place of worship, however, closed in 1937 when the latter died and ownership of the house passed into new hands.

In addition to providing a synagogue for worship, the Jewish community took care of many other needs of its members. From the moment a child was born, proper functionaries and facilities were made available. A *mohel* lived in Copenhagen at all times. A society *Chevra Kaddisha D'sanduko'us*, founded in 1810, gave financial help to the needy family in the first few weeks.[2] In addition, individual members of the community had established endowments for a variety of worthy causes since the eighteenth century. There were large endowments for the Jewish school, widows, travelers, the cemetery, *Kaddish*, old age homes, nursing and sick care, maintenance of the synagogue, wages for the rabbi and other religious functionaries, *klaus*, butter, meat and firewood. One of the most famous endowments was the Fund for Brides, established by Jacob Heyman Levy (brother of Moses Levy, founder of the synagogue in

---

[2] An account of the society and its many charitable activities was published on its 150th anniversary in 1960. A complete register of endowments (more than 400) was published in Copenhagen in 1878, with a supplement and a revision issued in 1890 and 1903, respectively.

Laederstraede). All these various charities were under the administration of the Jewish community and are still in existence today.[3]

The education of its youth has always been an important function of a Jewish community. In 1805 the Free Boys School was founded. It maintained a regular schedule of religious and secular studies. In the nineteenth century Jewish boys of all kinds attended this school. But at the beginning of the twentieth, boys whose parents had fled the pogroms in Russia and Poland began to predominate.[4] There was also a society to further the education of the graduates of the Boys School. The separate girls' school, Carolineskolen, which had been dedicated on Princess Caroline's birthday, October 28, 1810, was maintained by numerous endowments. Here, too, the students were taught secular as well as religious subjects. Home economics, sewing and cooking were part of the curriculum. The language of instruction in both schools was Danish, and in both the history and culture of Denmark was strongly stressed. The Jewish Boys School and Carolineskolen remained separate entities until 1943, when they were combined.

For those Jewish students who attended public or other private schools, the community maintained a *Religionskole* (established 1853), which was located in Fiolstraede. Instruction took place on Sundays and on weekday afternoons. Hebrew, Bible, Jewish history and religion were the subjects taught. Most of the teachers here came from other countries; no Hebrew teachers' seminary ever having been established in Denmark. Nevertheless, the teaching reflected the general attitudes of the Jewish community.

In 1922 a *cheder* was established by the *Machazekay Hadass* in Ole Suhrsgade. This school was conducted according to strict Orthodox tradition. Chumash with commentaries, Mishna, Talmud, Codes, Laws and Customs were taught to about twenty-five students. At least seven of these students later went to Polish and Lithuanian Yeshivoth to further their education. All of these

---

[3] Four additional funds for brides presently exist.
[4] Grethe Hartmann and Fini Schulsinger, *Physical and Mental Stress and Consequential Development of Atherosclerosis* (Copenhagen: Rosenkilde and Bagger, 1952), p.44: "The Jewish Boys' and Girls' schools, which were founded in 1805 and 1810, were thrown open to the children of the immigrants. . . ."

students, fortunately, returned to Denmark before the start of the Second World War.

A number of weekly study groups for adults were also to be found. The chief rabbi led a Talmud study group on Monday evenings and conducted a lecture series on the Prophets on Sabbath afternoons. There were regular sessions of the Rashi Society, where Rashi's commentary on the Bible was studied, and of the Etz-Chayim Association, which examined other Jewish subjects. Groups studying modern Hebrew and Jewish history were also active. In the home of Mrs. Winkler, the widow of Rabbi Winkler, who had ministered to the *Machazekay Hadass*, a weekly Talmud class was conducted which was always well attended. Considering the size of the Danish Jewish community, one cannot but be impressed by the many educational programs it offered.

The *klaus* or Talmud study group, was an old institution in Copenhagen; various *klauses* had existed here over the years. Early ones had been founded by Isak Jacob Moisling and by Raphael Asher Unna, whose last will and testament is dated June 10, 1798. It was customery for the rabbi or dayan, the shochtim and others well versed in the Talmud to participate in this group, in order "that a true house in the honor of God can be built, a place where the Talmud can be studied for all generations to come, . . . in order that the founder can have a share among those who do good for many." This most generous and religious man also willed money for *Kaddish* (to be recited on his day of death), to help poor brides to marry, to pay rent for the poor, to support the Free School for Boys, and for many other worthy Jewish causes.

The Jewish community early recognized the need for housing for the elderly infirm. Two old-age homes, the *Melchiors* and *Eibeschütz* foundations, were attached to the community center. There was a total of 38 free apartments in these homes. Two additional old-age homes were located in Copenhagen. *Meyer's Minde* and *Erkendligheden*, in back of the synagogue in Krystalgade, contained 28 apartments.[5]

---

[5] A number of years ago, these facilities were moved to a new building with more apartments in Utterslev, a suburb of Copenhagen.

All of these old-age homes were under the administration and supervision of the Jewish community. A private old-age home located in Dyrkøb, and known as *Joseph Frankel's Old-Age Home*, housed about eight persons. Anyone could, upon application, receive living quarters in any of these facilities. No distinction was made between applicants belonging to old Danish Jewish families and newly arrived immigrants from other lands.

A Jewish hospital was never established in Denmark, but there existed a Society for Nursing of the Sick, which provided much help and assistance. Numerous individuals willed money to this society.

The Jewish community's library was in Ny Kongensgade, where to this day its archives are stored. At the same location there is also a Jewish museum. Besides this library, mention must be made of the *Bibliotheca Judaica Simonseniana*, housed in the Royal Library. This collection, assembled by Professor David Simonsen over many years, contains numerous books of great value and interest, and has been an important resource to scholars from all over the world. The late Dr. Raphael Edelman, former librarian at the Royal Library - Jewish Division, has written extensively about this collection. In a scholarly article in Danish, he describes the library in detail, recounts the activities of Professor Simonsen, and assesses the importance of this collection to Jewish studies.[6]

Two *Chevra Kadisha* existed in Copenhagen, each of which had a long and proud history. *The United Israelitisch Burial Society* - known as the "Big Chevra" - was founded in Copenhagen on the 17th of Kislev 5619 (Nov. 24, 1858) through a union of two existing *chevros*, *Chovey Chesed* and *Lev Echad*, which had been established since the 18th century.[7] The "Little Chevra," or Society to Accompany the Deceased, was founded in January 1768. Its purpose was to insure that enough people would attend a funeral service and accompany the cortege. When this society celebrated its hundredth anniversary in 1868, it issued a memorial publication.

---

[6] R. Edelman, "David Simonsen," *Ved 150 Aarsdagen for Anordningen af 29 Marts 1814*, ed. Julius Margolinsky og Poul Meyer (København: A/S Oscar Fraenkel & Co., 1964), p.103.

[7] Julius Margolinsky (ed.) *Chevra Kaddischa 1858 - 1958* (København: A/S Oscar Fraenkel & Co., 1958), p.32.

Contained therein was an account of a man named Abraham Meyer (referred to as Abraham Strelitz) who kept a list of all funerals from 1771 until his death in 1796. This list provided out-of-town visitors with the location of all graves in the Møllegade cemetery. Previously, it had been difficult to find any grave in the cemetery.

Besides these two *chevros*, there was an organization called the Jewish Burial Society, founded in 1810. Any person of the Jewish faith could join this society, whereas in other chevros, only those who actually participated in their work could be members.

An early reference to a Copenhagen *Chevra Kadisha* is found in the volume *Shagas Aryeh v'Kol Shachal*, responsa number 19. The author of the volume, Rabbi Abraham Nathan Nota Meisels, head of the rabbinical tribunal in Vishnitz, relates that his grandfather, Rabbi Aryeh Leib ben Shmuel Zvi Hirsch of Brisk, then head of the rabbinical tribunal of Titkin, had received an inquiry from his uncle, Rabbi Simcha Katz Rappoport, head of the rabbinical tribunal of Lublin, pertaining to a shipwreck on the Swedish coast.

Rappoport referred to a document he had seen signed by three Jews of Copenhagen on the 28th of Tamuz 5453 (1693) regarding eight Jews who had drowned in the shipwreck. He also referred to testimony by a man in the city of Gothenburg, Sweden, who reported statements made by sailors to the effect that the ship including all men, women and merchandise had been lost at sea.

The question arising from this event concerned the right of the widows of the Jews who had drowned to remarry. It was answered in the affirmative. This responsum is most important because it is one of the first Hebrew sources on the Jews of Copenhagen.

One of the functions of the *Chevra Kadisha* was to assure that the two cemeteries in Copenhagen were maintained according to Orthodox Jewish tradition. The old cemetery in Møllegade dates from 1693, when a young man named David Israel died. It was impossible to bring his remains to Altona, where all Jews who had died in Denmark were previously buried. Four individuals who were officers of the congregation received permission form the municipal government of Copenhagen to bury the deceased outside the city walls. The following year a deed was issued to "the Jews who according to the status of July 30, 1684, had received citizens' rights to bury their deceased on this plot." This was the beginning of the cemetery on Møllegade.

Other Jewish cemeteries were located in Aalborg, Randers, Fredericia, Horsens, Odense, Faaborg, Assens, Slagelse and Nakskov. The oldest of these date from about 1710. No burials have taken place in any of these cemeteries for a number of years. They are, however, under the administration and supervision of the Jewish community of Copenhagen. Twice annually all are visited by representatives of the community to ascertain that graves and tombstones are in good condition.

In the middle of the nineteenth century, the community obtained a new cemetery – Western Jewish Cemetery – located on Vestre Kirkegaard. The first burial took place there in 1886. Serious problems faced the *chevra* with the institution of cremation and the wish to install an organ in the cemetery chapel. It was, however, already provided that in such cases where the family requested music at the funeral, officers of the *chevra* as well as their deputies must leave the chapel as long as the music was playing. The problem of cremation was solved by the *chevra* removing itself from funerals in which it was done. A special area of the cemetery was set aside for urns. The problems of urns was worked out in 1896 between the chief rabbi, Dr. Simonsen, and a representative committee of the community. It was decided that, upon request, the rabbi would attend the funeral of a cremated person provided the urn was placed in a casket of the usual size and shape. The first urn-funeral took place in 1893. In the decade 1893 – 1902 fourteen such funerals took place out of 568 regular burials.[8]

The women had their own *chevra*, which was closely tied to the nursing-service organization. The women's *chevra* took care of all cases which came to its attention in the most dignified and respectful way. As times changed, the membership in both the men's and women's *chevras* became divided into active members (who actually attended funerals, helped with the washing of the corpse, etc.) and passive members (who only paid their annual dues but did not

---

[8] By comparison, in the decade 1948 – 1957, the number had increased substantially. There were 143 urn-funerals to 515 regular burials.

participate in any of the sacred work). In 1958, the men's *chevra* had 125 active members and 97 passive members.

The women's *chevra*, for many years, had about ten active and about 160 passive members. Although numerous requests, both oral and written, were made to involve the passive members in the work of the organization on a voluntary basis, most of the time it had to be done by paid individuals from the Jewish community.

Numerous other *chevras* and societies existed in Copenhagen, each organized for a specific purpose. There was a society for Jewish youth to be placed in the arts and handicrafts (founded in 1795), a Love Thy Neighbor Society (*Ahavath Re'im*), a Danish chapter of *Alliance Israelite Universelle*, a society for the distribution of meat, firewood, and bread for travellers, and a chapter of *Chovevay Zion*, a Palestine settlement group, founded in 1897. All of these organizations had endowments to finance their work, and all of these endowments were, and still are, under the supervision of the Jewish community, and are administered by a special committee of the representatives.[9] In general, the Jewish community was guided in its daily work by a *representantskabet* (board of representatives) and a *delegeretforsamlingen* (assembly of delegates), the former being elected by the latter, who were elected by the community at large. Usually the most prominent and well-known Jews were found on the board of representatives. Elections of delegates took place every two years, and all who paid taxes to the Jewish community were eligible to vote.

The Jewish community was, of course, concerned for its youth. The largest youth organization was *Jødisk Ungdomsforening*, which maintained a variety of activities. The annual event that drew most participants, including ones from the other Scandinavian countries, was the summer camp, sponsored by all the Scandinavian Jewish Youth organizations. The site of the camp rotated between Scandinavian countries from year to year, and many lasting friendships were established among the young people. Obviously, no summer camp could be conducted after 1940, but festivities and

---

[9] A description of the foundations and the amount of the endowments has been issued periodically.

social events did not die out in the war years and were particularly in evidence at Chanukah and Purim. Frequently, the youth organization sponsored cultural events and discussions.

Although the youth organization was *the* organization for every young Jew or Jewess, its universality was shaded by the tendency of various groups of members—notably those born in Denmark, the Russian-Polish youth, and the German youth—to separate from one another. As Hartmann and Schulsinger put it, the Eastern European Jews "kept up the habit of isolation. They enjoyed being able to cultivate their cultural interest freely, which resulted in the foundation of a surprising number of clubs to further cultural, political, social and sports-interest."[10] To mention only a few, these organizations comprised *Hasomir* (a song club for men, which after 1945 included women), *Hakoah* (a sports club for men), a Jewish chess club, a Jewish bowling league, and the very active Craftsmen's Society—all of which had a membership of mostly Russian-Polish Jews. They were all active groups and clamored for recognition. When, on April 9, 1940, Denmark was occupied, they either toned down their activities or completely ceased. After the war, when these clubs were able to start again, numerous changes, particularly in the composition of their membership, were noticeable.

Another important organizaion, which engaged in many cultural and humanitarian activities, was the *Danmark Loge* (Denmark Lodge, B'nai B'rith, No. 712), established in 1912. When in 1962, the *Danmark Loge* celebrated its 50th anniversary, it published a book recounting its activities of the half century. Attached to the back of the volume were German and English synopses. Not all – but a majority of the lodge – were of the old Danish Jewish families. The lodge participated in a number of national and international fund-raising drives. In the 1930's the lodge was instrumental in bringing together three youth organizations, *Haivri Hazoir, Jeshurun* and Jewish Youth and combining them into the Jewish Youth Organization in 1934. In 1935 the lodge sponsored a cultural evening on the occasion of the 800th anniversary of the birth of Mai-

---

[10] *Physical and Mental Stress*, p.44.

monides. It was estimated that about three hundred guests attended this celebration. During the decade, 1933 – 1943 the lodge helped to bring some children to Denmark.

The lodge's interest in Zionism stemmed from the time of the Balfour Declaration of November 2, 1917, which resulted in two lectures by Georg Brandes on Dec. 4th and 10th of the same year.

The secretary of the lodge had, in a letter dated June 27, requested Georg Brandes to speak on a certain topic. In no uncertain terms he declined. A few months later, however, Brandes changed his mind; he had concluded his gigantic work about Julius Caesar, and declared himself available.

He started one lecture with the following words: "It is now more than twenty years that a man, unknown to me, Dr. Herzl, sent me a book which he called, no more, no less: *Der Judenstaat*. I left the book unopened. When he later pressed me for a comment I answered him jokingly with the following anecdote. Friedrich Wilhelm IV of Prussia asked the banker Mendelsohn what he thought about the king's idea to lead the Jews back to Palestine. In such case, answered Mendelsohn, I would like to become the new state's ambassador to Berlin! Herzl resented my improvident answer. He wrote me that most probably I could not imagine in what company I had placed myself by my answer. Twenty years have since passed and the unknown Dr. Herzl is right – while I, Georg Brandes, am totally wrong."

A number of professedly Zionistic organizations existed in Copenhagen. The oldest was *Agudath Hazionim b'Danmark* (*Dansk Zionistforening*), which was founded in 1902. There were also *Avodah*, the Zionist socialist organization, founded in 1930, *Mizrachi*, founded about 1907, *Hechaluz*, the Jewish pioneer organization, established in 1933, and *Bachad* (*Brith chaluzim datiim*), the religious pioneers, established a year later. It is impossible to ascertain how many members each of these organizations had, but it is estimated that the first three had a total membership of about 250.

The women had their own organizations. The Jewish Women's Organization was active in many philanthropic endeavors. It was especially helpful in providing homes for children who came to

Denmark in 1939. The Jewish Sewing Club, whose members came mostly from the *Machazekay Hadass*, met once a week to sew, embroider and do needlework. The objects they made were then sold at an annual bazaar. The monies they collected were then sent to needy Jews in East European countries, *yeshivoth* in Poland and Lithuania and religious settlements in Palestine.

Jews were kept informed about the acitivities of their fellow Jews by two publications, edited and published by the Jewish community. *Mosaisk Samfund* (Jewish Community) later called *Mosaisk Ugeblad* (Jewish Weekly) began publication in 1907 and ceased in April, 1940, because of the German occupation. *Jødisk Familieblad* (Jewish Family Paper), which began publication in 1928, also vanished in 1940. Both publications contained articles on current problems, schedules of synagogue services, personal announcements, organization news, book reviews, reports of meetings, and news from the international scene; and both were sent to all members of the community. After the war a new publication sprang up, currently called *Jødisk Orientering* (Jewish Orientation). A newspaper of the Scandinavian Jewish Youth Organization appeared in Copenhagen between April, 1936, and February 1940.

A yearly *Jødisk Almenak* (Jewish Almanac) was issued shortly before Rosh Hashono. However, it contained only a calendar. It was obtainable from the chief sexton, who was also in charge of selling *lulav* and *esrog* for the Succoth festival. There was no Jewish book store in Copenhagen; Jewish books and other religious articles had to be ordered from Germany or England. All such imports ceased with the outbreak of the Second World War.

However, even during the German occupation, matzohs were baked by the Jewish community for its members, while the *Machazekay Hadass* baked separately for its members. The Danish government readily made available flour for this purpose. No rationing coupons were required to buy matzohs.

It is also strange to record that *lulavim* and *esrogim* were obtainable in Copenhagen during the German occupation; these items were apparently imported from Yugoslavia. In contrast, when the Jews arrived in October, 1943, in neutral Sweden, they could find no lulav and esrog in the city of Malmö.

The Jewish community in Denmark was indeed self-sustaining in all regards. From its beginnings and throughout the many years of its growth and development, it had created institutions and endowments to provide for the needs and interests of every Jew on the social, educational, cultural and religious levels. In moments of joy the Danish Jew could count on fellow Jews to join him; in hours of distress he was assured of help, aid and comfort. As S. Friedman so beautifully expressed it: "Let us all—each according to his capabilities—walk in God's way. Whether we help the living ones, or we fulfill the last wish of a dear brother or sister, let us always remember, that for *G'milus Chesed* (acts of lovingkindness) no thank you is ever given or received."[11]

---

[11] Margolinsky, *Chevra Kaddischa*, p.31.

The interior of the Synagogue in Krystalgade. This magnificent edifice was dedicated in 1834.
Courtesy Arne and Helene Meyer

VI

Meir Goldschmidt and His Period

What were the social and cultural conditions of the Jews residing in Denmark at the time when the new constitution of 1848 was about to be ratified? Fortunately, there are writers of the time we can consult for specific answers. One of the Jewish community's own sons provides us with a magnificent picture of the hopes, aspirations, failures and successes which characterized both the Jewish and non-Jewish worlds of Copenhagen during this period of growth.

He is Meir Aaron Goldschmidt, the most important Danish-Jewish literary personality of the nineteenth century. Born in Vordingborg on August 15, 1819, Goldschmidt was the great-grandson of the founder of the Jewish community in Copenhagen. Jewish religious ceremonies were not observed in the home of his earliest years.[1] When he was six years old, he was sent to Copenhagen to attend school. There he lived with his strictly orthodox uncle, Hyman Josef Levine, and observed for the first time the practices of Judaism. The impressions he gained in Uncle Hyman's house remained with him for the rest of his life.

At the exclusive von Westers Institute, which he attended, Goldschmidt came in contact with the Danish intellectual community.[2]

---

[1] Poul Borchsenius, *Historien om de Danske Jøder* (Copenhagen: Det Hoffensbergske Etablissement, 1969), p.84.
[2] *Ibid.* p.85.

At the University of Copenhagen, he eagerly attended lectures on ethics and religion. During his undergraduate years he seriously considered being baptized. But he could not break with the Jewish tradition he had absorbed in his uncle's house. In the course of his oral examination at the university in 1836, his professor asked him a question from the catechism. Goldschmidt answered in an almost inaudible voice: "I am a Jew." The result was a poor grade. Discussing this incident with his contemporaries, Goldschmidt is said to have remarked: "To sympathize with defeat is not the hallmark of our race."[3]

Throughout his life and literary career, Goldschmidt, nevertheless, remained torn between two spiritual poles of belief. He never became a Christian, but he did not develop as a Jew, either. Understandably, one of his longest novels, which he wrote in 1853, is entitled *Hjemløs* (Homeless).

Goldschmidt expressed his conflict in numerous places in *Hjemløs*. During a lesson in physics, this dialogue between students and teacher occurs:

> "But yes," called one boy, "Aaron's rod was placed in the tabernacle, and in one night it got flowers and almonds."
>
> "And Jesus changed water to wine at the wedding in Cana," called another.
>
> The surprised and embarrassed teacher quickly answered: "Yes, but that was in those days before they had invented physics!"[4]

At another point in the book, Goldschmidt has two old student friends, Helzen and Mendoza, meet. Discussing the various kinds of arms with which one may fight a common political enemy, regardless of his nature, Helzen says:

> "You have the ability to fight, but you do not have arms. I battle with a sword, you with a prayer-candlestick."

---

[3] *Ibid*. p.82.
[4] M. Goldschmidt, *Hjemløs*, (Copenhagen: Gyldendalske Boghandel Nordisk Forlag, Vol. II, 1909) p.73.

"Now I know that," called Mendoza – "The artist is he who recreates a godly picture, and breathes into his work the spirit of life. . ."

"Surely it blows, Old Testament style" said Helzen.

"The artistic beauty within us, that is God," replied Otto.

"You at least speak like a good Christian, not that nonsense from the Old Testament."[5]

On another occasion, Goldschmidt tells about a Friday evening dinner. When the Jewish Sabbath starts, the observant Jew refrains from doing any manual work. Neither does he ask a non-Jew to perform any work for him. After having described the solemnity of the approaching Sabbath, the peaceful surroundings in the room, Goldschmidt lets his hero observe:

He turned down the lamp, without thinking about it at all. But by doing that, the strangeness that was between him and them became even clearer; they belonged to two different worlds. Even in the midst of their room, at their table, he was outside their family life.[6]

In 1845, Goldschmidt published his first novel, *A Jew*. In this work he portrays a young, gifted Jew, trained and educated in the orthodox Jewish tradition. During his years of study he attempts to leave his paternal faith. His mind is set on joining Christianity in order to be accepted at all levels of Danish society. Alternately drawn to this new faith and repulsed by it, Jacob Bendixen, the protagonist, is unable to find the proper place for himself. He carries on an internal battle, for he wants very much to be accepted. As the drama unfolds, he becomes spiritually more and more depressed. These strong opposing thoughts prey on his mind until he is finally destroyed.

Goldschmidt is obviously writing about himself throughout the book. The confrontation between Jacob and his uncle is probably also autobiographical.

[5] *Ibid*. p.154.
[6] *Ibid*. p.451.

> "Answer me son, did you eat ham?"
> Jacob's knees were shaking, but he answered: "Yes".
> A violent blow from the hand of his uncle hit him immediately at this confession. But in the next moment he made a decision. He left the room, the house, the city and walked away on the road. With obstinate thoughts he remained walking. . .[7]

At another time, when Jacob has a long and serious discussion with his friend Levi regarding their future plans, Jacob says:

> "My blood loves the Jews, but my spirit cannot live among them. It is a Christian spirit, and it seeks with extreme intensity its like."
> "Then become a Christian! Let yourself be baptized!"
> "Levi, you cannot mean this seriously. Let myself be baptized! Denying my past, my childhood, my whole being. . .it is a battle, and a greater battle than for my insignificant person. It concerns my people, my poor oppressed people!"[8]

At still another point, Jacob speaks about himself. He realizes that he is a Jew, but he seems to prefer to be a Christian. His aim is to discard his outer Jewish garments. Unfortunately he is not able to perform this act.

> "The Talmud states that one should learn to ride, fence and swim. I have learned these skills. I am a rider in Jewish garments. The disaster is only that I cannot discard this clothing."[9]

Jacob falls in love with a Christian girl named Thora. His friend, Levi, advises Jacob about the pitfalls attendant upon an interfaith marriage, which many Jews of Copenhagen, in the middle of the 19th century, saw as a means of gaining respectability and acceptance into the mainstream of Danish society.

---

[7] Goldschmidt, *En Jøde*, Vol. I, p.93.
[8] *Ibid.* p.116.
[9] *Ibid.* p.143.

"In marriage there is a religious element, whose spirit demands a higher unity between man and woman. But some hostility stands between Christianity and Judaism. I do not know from where this dark, indescribable hostility emanates."[10]

The final chapter of the novel deals with Jacob's burial. Everybody has left the cemetery after the religious services (which, incidentally, are described superbly), were conducted according to Jewish ritual. Only Levi remains. Folding his hands, he recites a brief prayer, then looks toward the city, where he had met Jacob as a young man, full of life. Levi says: "He once believed in eternal poetry and eternal life!"[11]

A Jew was well received by the general public. The book seemed to reveal something exotic, unknown and mystical about the Jews that lived among the Danes. The Jews of Copenhagen, however, felt insulted and were angered by it. To them it seemed a tasteless display of things they considered holy and sacred. Many years later, Georg Brandes, reviewing Goldschmidt's works, in typical Danish fashion, summed up these feelings: "He serves his grandmother in sharp sauce."[12]

Some of Goldschmidt's works, including *A Jew*, were translated in his day into English. In fact, *A Jew* appeared in two English versions, as Goldschmidt himself noted:

> In England, where *A Jew* was published in 1851. . . .peculiar circumstances were added. Two ladies translated the book simultaneously, Mrs. Bushby and Mrs. Howitt, the Quaker. The latter considered it appropriate "to adapt" my work according to English or her own taste. In the last chapter she baptized my Jew. But in the course of time Mrs. Bushby's more honest and less expensive edition won the competition. It is now sold as railway literature in England as well as in America.[13]

---

[10] *Ibid*. p.147.
[11] *Ibid*., p.284.
[12] Georg Brandes, *Samlede Skrifter*, Vol. II, (Kjøbenhavn: Gyldendalske Boghandels Forlag, 1900) p.453.
[13] Goldschmidt, Vol. VIII, p.207.

At barely twenty years of age, Goldschmidt became the editor of the weekly tabloid *Corsaren*. The first issue appeared on October 8, 1840.[14] Every Friday afternoon, this newspaper could be bought on the streets of Copenhagen. People were delighted by the satire and cynicism which appeared under the heading of "Charivari". Here Goldschmidt displayed a typical Jewish wit and humor (*chutzpa*) which became popular with all, except the unfortunate individuals who were the butt of it.

Søren Kierkegaard, the celebrated philosopher, became one of Goldschmidt's favorite targets. Kierkegaard actually invited the attack. In an article in *Faedrelandet*, of which he was the editor, Kierkegaard asked when it would be his turn to be castigated by "Charivari," as all respectable authors had been. Goldschmidt did not let the suggestion pass. Goldschmidt, in fact, admired Kierkegaard and the two had met numerous times. When, in 1843, Kierkegaard published his famous book *Either/Or* under the pen name Victor Eremita, Goldschmidt was so impressed with the work that he wrote in *Corsaren*: "The author of this book will be remembered eternally."[15]

But Goldschmidt's attitude towards Kierkegaard soon changed. As already mentioned, *A Jew* appeared in 1845 and received favorable notices from book reviewers. At one of their meetings, Kierkegaard asked Goldschmidt: "You have probably read the review of the book in *Faedrelandet*? What do you think is its meaning?" Goldschmidt said he assumed that Kierkegaard had praised his work. "No," said Kierkegaard, "the meaning is simple. There are people who will recognize you as the author of this book, but not as the author of 'Charivari.' The editor of your tabloid is P. L. Møller." Goldschmidt denied this. But Kierkegaard only smiled and, shaking his head, walked away.[16]

Thereafter, the attack in *Corsaren* started. Every week, articles and caricatures of Kierkegaard appeared. The paper pictured Kierkegaard as a small, hunchbacked individual, with thin legs and one

---

[14] Goldschmidt, Vol. I, p.2.
[15] Elias Bredsdorff, *Corsaren* (Copenhagen: Carit Andersen Forlag, 1941), p.50.
[16] *Ibid.*

trouser leg shorter than the other. It was especially this latter detail that people in Copenhagen considered most amusing. Kierkegaard's tailor was even accused of intentionally making the trousers uneven, though this was the invention of P. Klaestrup[17] who drew the caricatures.

One of Goldschmidt's most famous satires of Kierkegaard concerned the latter's "Thought Experiments."

"I will do something benevolent for the poverty-stricken of the city," Goldschmidt had Kierkegaard say. "I will think that I have given a poor woman with five small children one Rigsbankdaler. Now, imagine her joy! But think – think hard – about the five small innocent children seeing a real coin!!! That's a thought experiment!"

Kierkegaard responded with a violent attack in *Faedrelandet* in which he declared that *Corsaren* was a woman of easy morals. From then on *Corsaren* would not let up on him. Copenhagen enjoyed the feud immensely. People stopped in the street to look at Kierkegaard and his trousers. Kierkegaard could, of course, see the comical side of all this but he was nonetheless annoyed at being the butt of jokes for a society which did not understand what they were laughing about. He is supposed to have said: "I once thought that Copenhagen was a big city. Now I know that Copenhagen is a small village. And in a small village, one cannot live as in a big city."[18]

Goldschmidt remained the editor of *Corsaren* for six years. Following the issue of October 2, 1846, he sold the paper to M. Flinch for 1500 Rigsdaler, and soon thereafter the publication folded. Goldschmidt used the money to travel abroad "in order to get rid of the jokes and learn something." Thus ended the reign of terror of *Corsaren*.[19]

Goldschmidt's journey, lasting until October, 1847, took him to Hamburg, Leipzig, Vienna, Venice and Rome. On his way back he

---

[17] Peter Klaestrup (1820 - 1882), artist, was educated at the Academy for Fine Arts and at Lund's School for Painting. He drew for *Corsaren* and later for *Punch*. He also illustrated Holberg's *Peder Paars* and for Wessel's *Kaerlighed uden Strømper*.
[18] Villads Christensen, *Peripatetikeren Søren Kierkegaard* (Copenhagen: Graabrødre Torv's Forlag, 1965), p.38.
[19] Bredsdorff, p.55.

86 / *The Viking Jews*

met in Coppet the pastor of the Reform Church, named Pignet, a human being he felt understood him and responded to all his needs. "It is not only his words that made a deep impression upon me, but he himself had such a strong effect upon me, that I had the feeling that this was the personality about which everything could revolve."[20]

Goldschmidt had communicated impressions of his journeys in letters to his parents and sister. In Prague he was greatly astonished at the numerous Jews living there. His letter, which is dated November 11, 1846, rings with excitement:

> Can your fantasy conceive of this city of Jews with its 1200-year-old cemetery, and also the house where Lazarus Abeles killed his son, Simon, the way I have described it in my *Jew*. I have seen it in the Theinkirke where also Tycho Brahe rests.[21]

A few weeks later, Goldschmidt was in Leipzig. In a letter of November 2, 1846, he told his family about a meeting with a writer:[22]

> We greeted each other as Freemasons. Now I can find friendship among Jews any place in Germany, if I do not prefer Christians. In Vienna I will visit the Jewish "priest" Mannheimer from Copenhagen.[23]

Goldschmidt's uniqueness as an author is most evident in his novel *The Raven*, generally considered to be his best work. The novel relates the story of three brothers who emerge from the people to become refined personalities. The brothers fight against new and old social injustices, which are maintained and enhanced by powerful opponents and large financial institutions.[24] The theme of being a Jew in a non-Jewish society appears in this novel once again.

---

[20] Goldschmidt, Vol. I, p.4.
[21] Morten Borup, *Meir Goldschmidt's Breve til Hans Familie* (København: Rosenkilde og Bagger, 1964), p.126.
[22] *Ibid.*, p.124.
[23] Cf. Chapter IV.
[24] Goldschmidt, Vol. VI, p.160.

Speaking about charity, Simon Levi tells Mr. Krog that charitable foundations are a good investment. One donates money after his death, but uses it while alive. Mr. Krog asks whether such a high value is in fact placed on charitable contributions in Denmark. Are there really so few charitable individuals? Simon replies:

> "Few charitable individuals? I would not say that, Mr. Krog. On the contrary, all are charitable, and therefore it costs a good deal of money if it's to become noticeable."
> "Is that so," said Mr. Krog.
> "It is our invention," said Simon Levi.
> "Whose?"
> "Ours. You do know, Mr. Krog, that I am a Jew."[25]

In another place, two friends, Ferdinand and Ibald, observe Simon Levi as he walks at the edge of a forest, apparently looking for something he has lost. Nearby stands a donkey. Ibald asks Ferdinand if he has ever seen a raven ride a donkey?

"Well," says Ferdinand, "I suppose you mean a two-legged raven."

"What kind of a question is that," Ibald rejoins. "All ravens have two legs." To which Ferdinand replies:

> "That is also true. My raven is black, it has two legs, a large beak and can speak."
> "Where is that raven?"
> "There he goes and mumbles and gabbles."
> "Oh, it is the little black Jew. Does he steal. . .?"[26]

At the end of the story, Goldschmidt tells us what happened to Levi:

> We regret to say that Simon Levi did not become renewer of lottery tickets, but he has become the commissioner of the factory in Copenhagen. He often goes out there. When Ottilie sees him

---

[25] *Ibid.*, p.161.
[26] *Ibid.* p.397.

in the distance, she says smilingly to her husband: "There goes our raven." But one does not let him hear this, because he could misunderstand the reference to the black bird.[27]

The following year, Goldschmidt wrote a short story called "Maser – An Episode in the Life of Simon Levi." In the preface to this piece, Goldschmidt states that an editor of a newspaper wrote to him shortly after *The Raven* had appeared, asking for information about the peculiar events which overtook Simon Levi and his unmarried sister, Gidel, in the novel. The story, says Goldschmidt, is his answer.

One Friday evening, after dinner, Gidel is slumbering in a corner of the sofa and Simon is studying the holy Bible. They are poor people, but satisfied to live in peace. They do not expect great events to overtake them.[28] Goldschmidt pictures Levi bent over the book, reaching for cold peas and intermittently drinking a little beer, completely oblivious to his surroundings. This quiet and peaceful scene is interrupted by a knock at the door. Without looking up, Levi says: "Come in." He thinks it is the Christian neighbor coming to extinguish the lights, which Levi, being an orthodox Jew, cannot do on Friday night. There is another knock. Angrily Levi calls: "Come in, did you not hear me the first time?" A secretary of the Danish Foreign Ministry enters, informing the two elderly people, who are half awake, that Levi has inherited 200,000 Rigsdaler from a certain Phillips, recently deceased in Buenos Aires. What this news does to Simon and Gidel is superbly described by Goldschmidt. They have sleepless nights. Simon wracks his brains about the proper disposition of the inheritance. But being an observant Jew, he must first tithe away ten percent for charity (*maaser*). And that is 20,000 Rigsdaler, no small sum.

Levi is consumed by the problem. To whom should he give the money? Who needs it most? How might he gain – at the same time – a little honor and fame? People come to him for all kinds of worthy causes. His brother Mordcha, who calls himself Martin (it sounds

---

[27] *Ibid.* p.418.
[28] Goldschmidt, Vol. VII, p.149.

better in Copenhagen), until now the important member of the family, also asks for a "loan." His business is on the verge of bankruptcy.[29]

Levi has only donated a small part of tithe money to charity, when he begins to feel pangs of conscience. His brother's daughter is soon to be married. His sister Gidel needs an immediate operation. The surgeon comes to the house. He places all his surgical instruments on the dining room table. Watching these preparations, Levi sees him make the sign of the cross over the instruments. He asks what this sign means. The surgeon answers that he always makes this sign in the name of God when another person's health depends on his hand.

"A sign," says Levi. "Wait a moment before proceeding with the operation. I have some important business to attend to before you start." He goes into the next room, opens a drawer, and starts figuring out how much he still has to give away from the tithe money. But he knows the amount exactly. He only needs to make a decision. Impatiently, the doctor opens the door and says that he cannot wait any longer. Even though Levi may have to attend to important business, he must proceed with the operation. Levy closes his eyes. There is a grimace on his face. After a moment he says: "Now it is done!"[30]

Returning to the room where the sick Gidel is anxiously waiting for the operation to begin, Levi whispers into her ear that brother Mordcha will get the tithe.

"I have paid *maaser*. . . . Now you do not have to be afraid . . .and I am not afraid either."[31]

At his niece's wedding feast, the food is served and speeches are made. The first toast is made in honor of Simon Levi. Everybody knows that this feast is Simon's work. The great-grandchildren will still praise his name in the future. Overcome by tears of emotion, Levi feels something warm and soft against his cheek. It is the bride

---

[29] *Ibid.*, p.170.
[30] *Ibid.*, p.176.
[31] *Ibid.*, p.177.

embracing her uncle. And Goldschmidt concludes: "This happens to all who have no children."[32]

Goldschmidt's literary activities ended in 1887. He had written numerous letters, novels, short stories, plays, travelogues, romances, and impressions of places and people on his journeys. He used motifs from Denmark as well as from other countries. His settings are both urban and rural. His characters come from both the Jewish and Christian milieu. They come alive in political debates, religious ceremonies, personal encounters and philosophical considerations. The subject matters are manifold and multicolored.

His works, which total more than one hundred, are among the most significant in nineteenth-century Danish literature. His own philosophy, including his strong belief in a "nemesis," are most vividly expressed in his autobiography *Livserindringer og Resultater*, which appeared in 1877. In the introduction, Goldschmidt says that he was in no hurry to publish this work, because an autobiography can be explained and interpreted for or against the author until he dies. He wants to make the reader aware that the truth of his writings must be authenticated according to the rules of probability. Or to say it differently, "when one goes to a party, one can be well dressed, without giving the impression that one is wearing fake ornaments."[33]

"I am of the tribe of Levi" are the opening words of the autobiography. Proud words these for an author who, in a turbulent life, could never find his proper place. Torn between opposing religious convictions, he nevertheless reaffirms his roots in the priestly tribe of Levi, one of the twelve biblical tribes. This important fact permitted him to be called to the Torah in the synagogue before many others who were more learned in Judaism. Yet only once did he recite the ancient blessings. That was when he attained his thirteenth birthday and became Bar Mitzvah.[34]

He made his first discovery of hate as a boy in school. His teach-

---

[32] *Ibid.*, p.178.
[33] Goldschmidt, Vol. VIII, p.8.
[34] *Ibid.*, p.9.

er, Mr. Brygger, "who otherwise was a soft and pleasant individual," was speaking about England one day. Suddenly he said, 'this cursed thief.' It was not only the word but the sudden expression in his face which taught me like a revelation or order to hate."[35]

Goldschmidt describes in explicit detail the Jewish laws, ceremonies and holidays, which he learned about in his father's home but saw observed only in his uncle's. He loved the spirit of the Jewish holidays. He admired people who could live according to Jewish law, for whom religion was a way of life.[36]

He wanted the Christian world to accept the Danish Jew. Even at a mature age, Goldschmidt remained occupied with this problem. In a letter to his sister Ragnhild, dated June 29, 1884, he had told of a visit to Kissingen, a famous spa in Bavaria:

> One never sees a Christian and a Jew conversing. On my walks, I think I am the only one to greet and to be greeted by Christians and to speak with them. In the beginning I thought that the cold, determined, arm's-length antipathy also was directed towards me. After a while, the opportunity presented itself to people to ask my name, in the bathhouse, in the reading room and in the restaurant – and when I answered "Professor G. from Copenhagen," the faces melted. Now they say: Good morning professor. How do you do professor? and so on. It is not really the Jew they are against, but his mannerisms.[37]

But Goldschmidt could never make peace with his Jewishness. In one instance he says, "All my thoughts, my spirit, belong to the Christians." And in the next instance: "We are and will remain Jews, just as the Negro slave is and will remain black regardless of how much he will be emancipated."[38] This sense of an indelible Jewishness comes to him clearly as he stands at the arch of Titus in Rome and says: "Had I ever been able to forget that I am a Jew?"[39]

---

[35] *Ibid.*, p.31.
[36] *Ibid.*, p.41.
[37] Borup, Vol. II, p.135.
[38] Goldschmidt, Vol. 1., p.115.
[39] *Ibid.*, p.452.

He reviews his school days, his confrontation with Kierkegaard. Since he also offended public officials and politicians in his "Charivari," he was once fined and jailed.[40] Thus he became a martyr for the liberal element of Danish society. He was invited to the big national meeting on Skamlingsbanken[41] on March 11, 1848. Goldschmidt began his speech with the words, "I am a Jew, what do I want amongst you?"[42] Even here he sought to discover the difference between himself and other Danes, to resolve the inner conflict which tormented him all his life.

Regarding Palestine (Israel), Goldschmidt made this interesting observation:

> Earlier it always troubled me when I encountered opinions which maintained that Jews should return to Palestine. It seems to me that in such opinions lies a desire to expel us and consider us foreigners in Denmark. Now much has changed. If there is a call to gather all those who are scattered, and it becomes a real mission, then our youth, strengthened by the culture which they have attained, can emerge bright and strong. They will be dedicated youth. Love for one's religion does not necessitate hate for another religion. I think that I have seen Jewish children grow up to become such youth.[43]

Goldschmidt concludes his autobiography by restating his firm belief in nemesis. Life and death are the synthesis over which man has no power.[44]

Goldschmidt gives us our fullest picture of the cultural condition of the Jewish community in Denmark in the middle of the nineteenth century. His works provide the attentive reader with a wealth

---

[40] Goldschmidt, Vol. VIII, p.192.
[41] A hill in southern Jutland, approximately ten kilometers from the city of Kolding. Skamlingsbanken became a meeting place for the national movement in the matter of Slesvig-Holstein. In 1863 an obelisk was erected in memory to those who fell in the wars with Germany to keep Slesvig-Holstein Danish.
[42] Goldschmidt, Vol. VIII, p.201.
[43] *Ibid.*, pp.217-218.
[44] *Ibid.*, p.245.

of information otherwise unavailable in Danish-Jewish literature of the period. Yet it was not the external world but the inner landscape of the soul that Goldschmidt really sought to depict. The equality granted Jews in Denmark tended to blur the distinctions between themselves and other citizens. Members of the generation of Goldschmidt's parents had already ceased to practice Judaism in the home. And Meir Goldschmidt himself might have been entirely lost to Judaism but for the circumstance that he had spent formative years with an orthodox uncle. Even so, he lived his whole life, in a painful oscillation between the poles of Judaism and Christianity. Other Jews, less sensitive to their identity, resolved this crisis by allowing themselves to be baptized into the religion of the majority. Still others attempted to move into the mainstream of Danish society by entering into interfaith marriages.

VII

Interfaith Marriage

The subject of interfaith marriage forms a sad chapter in the history of Danish Jewry.

To set this subject in perspective, it is important to know something of the history of Jewish interfaith marriage in general. As Professor Nathan Goldberg has said, "The attitude of the twentieth-century European, American and other Jewish men and women towards interfaith marriage is not the same as that of their ancestors. . . . At one time they were admonished that whoever gives 'his daughter or his sister to any man who is of the seed of the Gentiles he shall surely die, and they shall stone him with stones. . .and they shall burn the woman with fire.' Whether or not the death penalty was ever inflicted on such transgressors, the traditional attitude has been against such marital unions. The present century, however, has witnessed an upward trend in interreligious marriage in European, American and other Jewish communities. And they have a more tolerant attitude toward those who out-marry than their forebears."[1]

This certainly is applicable to the situation in Denmark. As interfaith marriages have steadily increased the attitude of the Danish-

---

[1] Federation of Jewish Philanthropies of New York, Commission on Synagogue Relations, *Proceedings of a Conference: Intermarriage and the Future of the American Jew*, New York, December 1965, p.27.

Jewish community has changed, both in respect to the relationship between parents and child, and between the community at large and the intermarried person. This change has also been noted by Professor Goldberg: "The parents, no matter how strenuously opposed they are to such marriages, tend to forgive their children for acting contrary to their will. The Jewish community tolerates such individuals. In brief, the attitude toward those who out-marry has undergone a radical change."[2]

In Denmark it is quite common to find families of which both the second and third generations have married outside the faith. There even are cases of completely intermarried families, whose only remnant of Judaism is the family name. Although the "new" partner in an interfaith marriage might not be accepted immediately, opposition soon decreased, and the latter would eventually be considered a full-fledged member of the family. It should be understood, however, that interfaith marriages in Denmark rarely came about because of social pressure, economic advantage or political expediency. The Jews had complete freedom in all endeavors. Rather, such marriages were a direct result of the liberal attitude of the Danes towards their fellow citizens of the Jewish faith. And the Jewish community in Copenhagen responded in kind, withholding from the "new" individuals only such specifically religious benefits as burial in the cemetery.

Throughout most of history, interfaith marriages have been opposed by all segments of Judaism. In an article on "Intermarriage and the Survival of the Jewish People," Meir Ben Horin declared that "Judaism, in order to live, must require the fullest loyalty to itself on all levels of homebuilding or Zionist realization."[3] Furthermore, Jews must possess the resolve to build homes, Jewish homes,. . . "those little Zions, from which there goes forth the law, the little Jerusalems from which breaks forth the Word of the Lord calling upon us to move forward from one Zion to the next."[4]

---

[2] *Ibid.*, p.34.

[3] Meir Ben Horin, "Intermarriage and the Survival of the Jewish People," *Intermarriage and Jewish Life*, ed. Werner J. Cahnman (New York: The Herzl Press, 1963), p.49.

[4] *Ibid.*

The Jews of Denmark were not greatly interested in building those "little Jerusalems." In Denmark one was born a Jew, attended a school which provided some Jewish education, and was thereafter left to oneself. If the home did not exert a strong Jewish influence upon the child, chances were that, sooner or later, he would enter into an interfaith marriage. The facts speak for themselves. There was never really a Jewish neighborhood or Jewish street in Copenhagen. The Jews literally lived among the Danes, both in the capital city and, earlier, in the provincial cities. There was no place where a Jew could not go, no event he could not attend. He was readily admitted everywhere. "Interfaith marriage," says Professor Goldberg, "implies a willingness on the part of the members of different religious communities to become marital partners. This is likely to occur when the groups do not raise any serious religious, social, political or other objections to such marriage or when members of religious groups are willing to ignore the societal regulations relating to the selection of a spouse."[5] This was exactly the case of the Danish Jew. No serious objections were raised on either side, and scant consideration was given to the choice of a marriage partner on religious grounds.

One may ask whether this situation was unique to Denmark or whether interfaith marriages have been accepted in other countries as well. If we look to Switzerland, which is also one of the smallest countries in Europe, a similar picture emerges. An article on "Interfaith Marriage in Switzerland" reveals that: "The Jews never accounted for more than ½ of 1 percent of the total population. . . . The intermarriage of Jews with those of other faiths has been steadily increasing in Switzerland, and is probably representative of the experience in other countries where the process of acculturation has continued over a considerable period of time."[6] Some important differences, however, should be noted. The Swiss have never been too liberal in extending citizenship to foreigners. Even children are not accorded citizenship at birth in Switzerland if their parents hap-

---

[5] Commission on Synagogue Relations, p.47.

[6] Jacob Baar and Werner J. Cahnman, "Interfaith Marriage in Switzerland," *Intermarriage and the Survival of Jewish Life*, ed. Werner J. Cahnman (New York: The Herzl Press, 1963), p.53.

pen to be aliens. In Switzerland, whose population is both Catholic and Protestant, Jews who have married outside the faith have showed a considerably greater preference for Protestant over Catholic spouses.[7] In Denmark there are very few Catholics, and the chance for a Danish Jew to intermarry with a Catholic is practically non-existent. But there is a similarity between the Jews of Denmark and the Jews of Switzerland in that both enjoy economic, civil and religious freedom. And as Professor Goldberg writes, "a correlation [exists] between the acculturation of the Jews and their willingness to have a non-Jewish marital partner."[8]

Let us now consider the situation in Denmark in specific detail. In 1682, seven Jewish families, consisting of nineteen people, resided there. Forty years later (1722) we find the number grown to sixty-five families with 350 persons. The increase of the Jewish population over the next one hundred and fifty years, as well as its movement toward Copenhagen, can be observed in Table 1.

Table 1[9]
Jewish Population 1840 – 1921

	Jews	% of total population	Jews in Copenhagen	% of all Jews in Copenhagen
1840	3839	0.29	2248	58.6
1845	3670	0.27		
1850	3941	0.28		
1855	4143	0.28		
1860	4214	0.26	2858	67.8
1870	4290	0.24		
1880	3946	0.20	3030	79.2
1890	4080	0.19	3264	85.6
1900	3476	0.14	2826	81.3
1911	5164	0.18	4710	91.2
1921	5924	0.17	5875	99.2

[7] *Ibid.*, p.55.
[8] Commission on Synagogue Relations, p.45.
[9] *Zeitschrift für Demographie und Statistik der Juden* Vol. 9 (1913), p.47. The last three lines from: *Die Juden in Dänemark, Zeitschrift, 1924*, Neue Folge, p.29.

The percentage of the "old" Jewish families of the total population of Copenhagen was, in 1789, 1.9%; in 1885, 2.3%, and by 1952 had dropped to 0.2%. After the First World War the number of the old families steadily declined and, as Julius Margolinsky states, "by 1945 there were less than 1500 persons.[10] This figure, however, does not tell us anything about how many family members and their children had left the Jewish community and been integrated into the Danish community; it merely tells us how many remained loyal to the Jewish community by marrying within the faith.

As previously stated, permission for the first Jewish interfaith marriage was granted by the government in 1798. Since then a gradual increase in such marriages occurred over the years. However, they did not assume significant proportions until the latter half of the nineteenth century. Cordt Trap in his 1922 study gives the following figures for old Danish-Jewish families, based upon the census of 1921.

Table 2[11]
Marriages Among Danish Jewry

Year	% Interfaith Marriage	% Jewish Marriage
1906	33.9	66.1
1911	41.4	58.6
1916	44.3	55.7
1921	51.7	48.3

The tendency toward interfaith marriage continued into later years. Julius Margolinsky, in his statistical resume, showed that this tendency existed not only up to the Second World War but also during the German occupation of Denmark and among the Danish Jews in Sweden in the years 1943 - 1945. The data further show that 60% of members of the Danish-Jewish families in Sweden who married entered into interfaith unions. Perhaps some might argue

---

[10] Julius Margolinsky, *Statistiske Undersøgelser over Flygtninge fra Danmark*, Stockholm, 1945, p.8.

[11] Cordt Trap, *Russische Juden in Kopenhagen*, (Zeitschrift für Demographie und Statistik der Juden, Neue Folge, 1926, vol. 3), p.4.

that the situation was different, that the problems were greater during the sojourn in Sweden. Yet, in the period 1945 – 1949, after the Danish Jews had returned to Denmark, the number of interfaith marriages performed comprised exactly the same percentage—60%.[12]

While the Danish Jews lived in Sweden (1943 – 1945) a total of 120 marriages were contracted. Following is a statistical abstract of these unions.

Table 3[13]
Marriages Among Jews From Denmark 1943 – 1945

	Number of Marriages	%
Old Danish Families. All Jewish	8	6.7
Old Danish Families. One spouse non-Jewish	12	10.0
Russian Immigrants and their children, all Jewish	33	27.5
Russian Immigrants and their children, one spouse non-Jewish	40	33.3
German Immigrants. All Jewish	17	14.2
German Immigrants. One spouse non-Jewish	10	8.3
Total	120	100.0

A somewhat different study was made by Julius Margolinsky of Danish Jews during the time they resided in Sweden. (Unfortunately, this study has not yet been published in full.) Basically, it reveals that the total number of people of Jewish extraction who fled Denmark, including "half-Jews," was 7,220. The "official" Jewish population of Denmark in October, 1943, was 6,383, including the 475 individuals who were deported to Theresienstadt, the German concentration camp in Bohemia. Approximately 50 to 100 Jews remained in Denmark during the twenty-two months that the rest were in Sweden. These either stayed "illegally," or lived with non-

---

[12] Jødisk Samfund, January 1950, p.20.
[13] *Statistiske Undersøgelser*, p.23.

Jews in a manner the Germans did not consider dangerous or subversive. But the greatest part of Jews living in interfaith marriages did flee to Sweden. A total of 936 couples of differing faiths were registered with the Danish Refugees Office in Stockholm. Of these, 583 of the husbands and 353 of the wives were Jewish; 512 non-Jewish women and 174 non-Jewish men accompanied their Jewish marriage partners to Sweden.[14]

Of the 6,383 Danish residents counted as Jews in 1943, 1,561 belonged to the old Danish-Jewish families, 3,340 were mostly Russian and East European immigrants or their descendants who had settled in Denmark at the beginning of the twentieth century, and 1,482 were refugees from Germany, Austria and Czechoslovakia who had arrived in Denmark after 1933.

Nineteen years later there were approximately 6,200 Jews in Denmark (all included). Between 1954 and 1963, 527 children were born and 683 members died. Yet, Margolinsky maintained that one must note this decline in the birthrate with caution. The situation is quite different nowadays than it was earlier in the twentieth century, when apathy and indifference were rife in the Jewish community. Various events which have taken place in Israel and elsewhere in the world have rendered the situation more complex.

---

[14] Julius Margolinsky, "Det jødiske Folketal i Danmark efter 1814," *Ved 150 Aars-Dagen for Anordningen af 29 Marts 1814*, ed. Julius Margolinsky og Poul Meyer, (København: A/S Oscar Fraenkel & Co., 1964) p.209.

VIII

The Period After 1849

The new Danish Constitution, which replaced the old Danish Law of 1665 was ratified by the United Danish Parliament on the 25th of May 1849 and signed by King Frederick VII on June 5th of that year. The constitution was a rather short but concise document, which granted equality to all citizens, regardless of social position, class or sex. It was, of course, written in Danish, but an exact and complete translation in English was prepared for the Danish colonies in the West Indies.[1]

Certain provisions in the document relating to the Jews had actually been passed into law earlier the same year. For example, on February 2, 1849, a statute was enacted regarding the registration of weddings, births and deaths. Anyone neglecting to comply with this statute had to pay a fine to the officers appointed to keep the official record.[2]

On February 18, 1849, another statute modified the law of March 29, 1814, in regard to the election of the Jewish community's board

---

[1] *The Constitution or Fundamental Law for the Kingdom of Denmark.* As passed by the United Diet on the 25th of May 1849, approved and sanctioned by His Majesty Frederic the Seventh, June 5, 1849. St. Croix, Christiansted, undated, 6 pages.
[2] O. A. Borum, *Dansk Lovsamling 1665 – 1891* (Copenhagen: G. E. C. Gads Forlag, 1931), p.417.

102 / The Viking Jews

of representatives. Henceforth the community was to be guided by seven representatives, freely elected by all members.[3]

This statute, furthermore, specified many fine points pertaining to the election. A father and son, or a father-in-law and a son-in-law could not serve on the board simultaneously. Any man or woman who possessed citizenship, was 25 years of age or more and paid taxes to the community was entitled to vote. The final paragraph abolished the requirement that at least one of the representatives should belong to the Portuguese community.

The Jews, thus having received official equality with the rest of Danish society, were eager to make their contributions to the good and welfare of the state. The spirit of humanity which permeated the new Constitution resulted in Jews now settling in the provincial cities. There they established prominent businesses and important factories. The community in Randers, Jutland, grew significantly in the second half of the nineteenth century. The families residing there created and shared a true Jewish communal life, crowned in 1858 by the opening of Randers' own synagogue. The spiritual leader and rabbi, Dr. Meyer Abraham Wreschner, was described by the late Chief Rabbi Friediger as "a dynamic personality, who knew how to gain the trust, admiration and respect of the community."[4]

Also in Aalborg, Jutland, a Jewish community was growing. In 1854, the synagogue was dedicated there. It was headed by Salomon A. Mielziner, who had come from Germany and served as the rabbi for forty years.[5]

In Faaborg, Fyn, Rabbi L. M. Wallach ministered to the Jewish population for almost fifty years. He came from Rendsborg, Germany, was a well-educated leader, and also taught languages at the public high schools.

But it was the Jewish community of Copenhagen that developed most significantly on the political, economic and social levels. Jews also made valuable contributions to the arts and sciences. As M. L.

---

[3] *Ibid.*, p. 418.
[4] Max Friediger, *Jødernes Historie* (Copenhagen: P. Haase & Søns Forlag, 1934), p.357.
[5] *Ibid.*

Nathanson informs us, "from 1848 to 1858, eighteen persons were granted the order of Ridder of Danneborg, two among them 'priests,' namely Dr. Wolff and the former Kateket for the island of Fyn, Cohen. Awards for various achievements were made without regard to religious conviction."[6]

In the political arena, the Brandes brothers became prominent. Georg Morris Cohen Brandes was born in Copenhagen on February 4, 1842. Although he travelled extensively during his lifetime, he remained a Danish Jew, but without religious conviction. He grew up in a completely irreligious home. A story is told about Georg Brandes, when as a young boy one day he took a walk, and someone called him a Jew. When he returned home, he asked his mother what the word meant.

"Jews," said his mother, "are certain types of people." The boy continued to ask: "Are they ugly people?"

"Yes," answered the mother, "sometimes quite ugly, but not always."

"Can I ever see a Jew?" asked the boy. Whereupon the mother lifted him up in front of a mirror and said: "That is a Jew."

The child screamed and the mother quickly put him back on the ground. She regretted forever afterward not having prepared her son for life as a Jew. This recorded incident reflects the condition of a growing segment of Danish Jewry.[7]

Georg Brandes studied at the University of Copenhagen. Upon graduation he received the university's gold medal for excellence in all studies. His hope was to teach ethics at the university. But his being born Jewish made it impossible for him to find a proper place both within the academic community and Jewish society. Torn between his loyalties, he thought about baptism, and finally declared himself a "citizen of the world." The contemporary writer Henri Nathanson said about Brandes: "The Jew that he was he did not want to be, and the Dane that he wanted to be he was not."[8]

---

[6] M. L. Nathanson, *Historisk Fremstilling af Jødernes Forhold og Stilling i Danmark*, (Copenhagen: Berlingske Bogtrykkeri, 1860) p.243.
[7] Poul Borchsenius, *Historien om de Danske Jøder*, (Copenhagen: Det Hoffenbergske Establissement, 1969) p.113.
[8] *Ibid.*, p.117.

104 / The Viking Jews

Georg Brandes became a literary critic and wrote prolifically. He reviewed Danish as well as foreign works, and travelled to numerous places in Europe, from which he gained insight, understanding and wisdom. His writings in Danish, indeed, form a rich collection of personal observations, critical analyses, political ideas, addresses speeches and poetry.

To Brandes, Judaism, the Jewish people, and the Zionistic idea were all matters without personal interest or attachment. Elias Bredsdorff rightfully points out that whereas Nathanson cultivated Jewishness, Brandes derided it: "Judaism" he said mockingly.[9] One does not find in his work a shred of the pride in his ancestral faith which characterized Goldschmidt.

All 18 volumes of his collected works bespeak the attitude of the assimilated Danish Jew at the end of the nineteenth century. Brandes was a Dane before all else. "I love the Danish language," he said. "I have always been most observant and careful to write as clearly and precisely as possible."[10]

As a Dane, he felt he could be critical of Denmark and wrote that "It is a disaster to have been born in such a small and weak country."[11] And in a letter to Edmund W. Gosse, dated February 13, 1877, he complained about the Danish people, whom he called "dreadful, pitiful, tragic and stupid. I get gray hair thinking about all the ignorance and selfishness which is in Denmark."[12]

Reviewing Goldschmidt's writings, Brandes called them the work of a master. Nevertheless, he considered it tasteless of Goldschmidt to discuss Jews and Jewish subjects continuously. "I can find no charm in an author continuously returning to the fact that he is a Jew," he wrote.[13] Goldschmidt "ought to let the mysteries of Judaism rest."[14]

[9] Elias Bredsdorff, "Georg Brandes as a Fictional Character," *Scandinavian Studies*, 45/1 (Winter 1973), p.13.
[10] Georg Brandes, *Samlede Skrifter* (Kjøbenhavn: Gyldendalske Boghandels Forlag, 1899), Vol. I. p.3.
[11] *Correspondance of G. Brandes*, (ed.) Paul Krüger, Letter to Edmund W. Gosse, dated June 3, 1884 (Copenhagen: Rosenkilde og Bagger, 1956), p.288.
[12] Ibid., p.83.
[13] Brandes, Vol. II, p.453.
[14] Ibid.

Yet Brandes was not insensitive to the uniqueness of Goldschmidt's contribution.

> He continuously loved two nationalities more than any other . . . the Jewish and the Danish. He considered himself as a sort of noble-born bastard, like the bat in the fable who said to the mice: "Look I am a mouse" and to the birds: "Look I have wings." He aimed to make his contribution to an answering of the question: what is the mission of the Jew in a modern culture.[15]

In his own writing about Jews, Brandes could be so removed as to find virtue in anti-Semitism. He spent several years (October 1877 to February 1883) in Germany, where he encountered a noticeable intellectual and religious movement against the Jews. He was not disturbed, however. In an essay dated January 17, 1881, he wrote:

> If this [German] movement would force the Jews into a strict and hard self-criticism, if it could impress upon them that they more than anybody else ought to watch their lives, their dealings – because so many are made responsible for an individual's mistakes and offences, if they could say to themselves that one Jewish loanshark can create many more catastrophes than another [gentile loanshark], and that a Jewish swindler, libertine or fool will bring shame and sorrow over all his co-religionists; if they only could hear one voice above all the shouts against them – a multi-tongued suggestion for hard work, seriousness, quiet behavior, manly strength for a renewed and increased love of freedom, philanthropy, charity for the poor and oppressed of all races; if, in brief they only could tell themselves and one another again and again, that a history enobles, that a responsibility ennobles, and that nobility obliges – then will even this soulless and impure movement not disappear without having borne good and remaining fruit.[16]

Brandes' discomfort with his Jewishness went back to his childhood days, which have strikingly been recalled by A. Hagensen.

---

[15] *Ibid.*, p.454.
[16] *Ibid.*, p.278.

106 / The Viking Jews

As a child he felt oppressed by belonging to this "despised, cursed, ugly and homeless people." His position could not be paralleled to a poor boy among rich, or an illegitimate child among legitimate, nor a Catholic among Protestants, not even a crippled among properly developed boys. Because the Jewish boy, in a Christian school of the old type, felt something that each of these marked ones feel and something additional still, to which they are not exposed. He learned for the first time, that he was a Jew, all that is contained within the framework of this word.[17]

Yet, though he wished to cease being a Jew, Brandes in his heart knew that this was not entirely possible. "Why," he asked, "is it that paving stones on which one has walked when young stick to one's feet. Why do they prevent one from rising and flying away?"[18]

Brandes was most sensitive about being reminded that he was a Jew. After a long period of animosity and silence, Brandes wrote the Danish writer, Holger Drachman, a letter dated November 3, 1891, recalling the fact that Drachman was the leader against him of

the Danish movement against me, to have me made into a stranger, a Jew. I can of course pardon – as it is called. For one pardons out of pride. But forget! How can I ever forget?[19]

In his introduction to a long discussion of nineteenth-century literary movements, Brandes informs the reader that "thoughts of reformation emanate from Germany and thoughts of revolution from France." He then goes on to compare the Danish language to a little church with a small altar, his images coming from Christianity, not Judaism. "Our literature [Danish] is like a little chapel in a huge church. It has its altar, but the high altar is not found there."[20]

In his essay *Kamp mod protestantiske Fordomme*, Brandes maintains that the Italian Renaissance stripped Christianity of its

---

[17] A. Hagensen, *Den Jødiske Periode, 1864 – 1900* (Kjøbenhavn: E. Jespersons Forlag, 1901), p.46.
[18] Brandes, Vol. III, p.125.
[19] Morton Borup, *Breve fra og til Holger Drachman* (Kjøbenhavn: Gyldendals – Nordisk Forlag, 1970), Vol. III, p.452.
[20] Brandes, Vol. IV, p.3.

"sense of renunciation," of its entire Jewish-Asiatic garb, and changed it to a beautiful, flower-decorated and incense-smelling mythology.[21]

But Brandes was not happy with Christianity either. In a letter to Henrietta Stradtmann, dated January 1, 1876, he says that barely five years earlier he rarely entered a Jewish home.

> Now, since I have attacked Christianity, nearly all Christians are afraid of me. [They are] either half or false friends. I have abandoned them, and now I associate with more Jews than Christians.[22]

In 1897, Brandes wrote some short essays about various countries. One of these essays dealing with Denmark is entitled *Farum*.[23] In this piece, Brandes tells us that when he was ten years old, he was sent for the summer vacation to a teacher in Farum, a small Danish village. There he met two girls, Henriette, blond, aged ten, and her sister, Nina, who had pitch black hair and was eight years old. Both had come from Brazil to spend the summer in Farum. The next day the three of them meet a boy named Per, who called Brandes a Jew from Copenhagen. This led to a fistfight between the boys which Brandes won. The following day, Henriette came to Brandes with two leather straps. She asked him if he would let himself be bound. He agreed and she tied him up with one of the straps. Then she proceeded to beat him with the other strap. After he had received many stripes and his beautiful jacket was torn to pieces, she untied him. He had neither cried nor screamed, nor asked for mercy. Now he only looked at Henriette in great amazement. The story ends: "This was the first time that I learned about feminine cunning."[24]

In his essay on *Rumania* Brandes remarks that the European country where oppression of the Jews is most severe is Russia. Twenty years ago, he says, the mass expulsion of Jews caught the attention of the world. Those that remain are being mistreated in

---

[21] *Ibid.*, p.149.
[22] Nolin, p.125.
[23] Brandes, Vol. XI, p.261.
[24] *Ibid.*, p.263.

every possible way. A rival to Russia in the persecution of Jews is Rumania. On entering Russia, Brandes observes tersely, any traveller will notice three things: the language, which does not resemble any Western European language; the Russian alphabet; and the computation of time. With respect to the latter, the traveller will be torn away from his accustomed calendar. He must turn the clock back twelve days. "I wish," concludes Brandes wryly, "that Russia were only twelve days behind Europe."[25]

Despite his consciousness that Jews were oppressed, Brandes continued to stand outside the Jewish community. On December 26, 1883, he wrote Paul Heyse as follows: "This year my wife prepared a beautiful Christmas for the children. Now they are old enough to enjoy the holiday and the gifts."[26]

Yet on a visit to the United States in 1914, while being interviewed by a reporter for *The American Hebrew*, he declared:

> It is ridiculous to say that I deny my ancestry. I have been attacked all my life as a Jew and because I am a Jew, I cannot forget nor deny that I am Jewish, even if I wanted to. Can anybody refuse me the name "Jew" because I do not frequent the synagogue? But I do not go to any church. I am not religious.[27]

Brandes' attitude towards Zionism and Palestine was one of unconcealed contempt.

> Now Zionism insists that it is a nation, and as a nation it needs a state. With spokesmen like the mediocre Max Nordau, the whole idea becomes most obnoxious. Furthermore, they [the Zionists] give loud assurance that hatred for the Jews will never die. A Jew that calls himself a Frenchman or Englishman is a contemptuous person who denies his brothers. It is only natural that the great Jewish financial dynasties divorce themselves from this movement . . . which is so illogical and clumsy.[28]

---

[25] *Ibid.*, p.456.
[26] Paul Krüger, Vol. III, p.282.
[27] Julius Moritzen, *Georg Brandes in Life and Letters* (Newark, N. J.: D. S. Colyer, 1922), p.89.
[28] *Ibid.*, p.486.

All he could say in favor of Zionism was that it might produce a Palestine "cultivated like a garden, and inhabited by a few million well-educated and thrifty Jews providing a haven for those of their co-religionists whose country of birth has nothing to offer to them."[29]

In one of his speeches, Brandes defined his religion. Addressing a group of students attending a political meeting in Hansted Skov in 1886, he asked: "What is our religion," and he answered his own question with these words:

> We love and honor freedom too much for us to ever call it by name. Not only do we honor it, but as I said, it is our religion. We worship it, we pray to it, and we bring its message to the world at large. We disseminate it as a force in whose beneficial effect we trust.[30]

In all his attitudes and writings Brandes revealed himself as a completely assimilated Danish Jew, one who could find no redeeming values either in being a Jew, or being a spokesman for the Jewish condition. Although his literary works are a part of the classic Danish canon, his contribution to Danish Jewry has to be written off as minimal.

Yet Henri Nathansen in his book *Georg Brandes – Et Portraet* sums up Brandes as follows:

> But a stranger he was – of course, he was a stranger. In nature and spirit, in thought and feeling, in instinct and temperament. His blood and nerves were Jewish. Perhaps the most distinct Jewish personality not only in his country, but in his time.[31]

Georg's brother, Edward, born in 1847, was a philologist and a journalist. In 1880 he became active in politics as a candidate for parliament for Langeland county, a small island south of Zealand. The election campaign was primarily a test of personality. How could he, a Jew, freethinker and academician represent the farm-

[29] Brandes, Vol. XII, p.268.
[30] *Ibid.*, p.269.
[31] Henri Nathansen, *Georg Brandes – Et Portraet*, (Kjøbenhavn: Nyt Nordisk Forlag, 1929) p.99.

ers? The opposition tried to pin the label of atheist on him, and to make the matter worse, on election day, he publicly declared that he did not believe in the Jewish or Christian God. When he won the election a stormy debate ensued. How could an avowed atheist become a member of parliament? How could he sign the oath which ended, "so help me God"? Brandes vehemently objected to any investigation of his personal beliefs, stating that his only obligation was to uphold the laws and the Constitution. It was then that the priest, Chresten Berg, declared, "The Danish parliament, is according to its composition and creation undenominational, is not based on the national church, but is a pagan house, and nothing else."[32] Later, Edward Brandes co-founded the daily newspaper *Politiken*, to which he contributed literary articles. In the year 1900 he became involved in a duel with a young artist, for which both received a prison term of fourteen days. At the beginning of the twentieth century he accepted a post in the government of Zahle. He died in 1931.

In the economic sphere, a number of Jews went into the banking business. David Baruch Adler, born in 1826, co-founded the Privatbanken in 1857. He was only twenty-eight years of age when he became director of the new bank. The older C. F. Tietgen, who headed the bank for more than forty years, could not tolerate a young Jew in so important a position. The conflict resulted in Adler's departure. But he remained convinced that he would be a success in banking. He worked diligently to establish a new bank, Handelsbanken, in 1873. He did not however, live long enough to reap the fruits of his labor. At 52 years of age he passed away, and was buried in the old cemetery on Møllegade. Adler remained faithful to the Jewish community, a member of its Reform wing.[33]

A strange financial wizard was Gottlieb Hartvig Abrahamson Gedalia. Grandson of the former chief rabbi of Denmark, he was born in 1816 in a poor neighborhood of Copenhagen, attended the Free Boys School, and at age thirteen became apprenticed to an upholsterer. But he had greater ambitions in mind. Every evening,

[32] Borchsenius, p.166.
[33] *Ibid.*, p.180.

after work, he dealt in stocks and bonds. In 1848 he applied to the municipal authorities for a broker's license. On May 1, 1849, he advertised in the daily newspaper, *Berlingske Tidende*, that he had opened an office on Højbroplads, across the street from the stock exchange.[34] Working diligently, he piled up money. Every day he went to the stock exchange, and he soon became the most talked about person in the city. For 12,000 lire he bought himself a letter of nobility as baron of San Marino. Then he became Portuguese consul general of Denmark. He liked uniforms and medals. In 1871, he started a bank, Landmandsbanken. The board of directors consisted mostly of wealthy farmers, who were eventually able to have him removed. Gedalia thereupon entered the railroad building business. He wanted to connect the two Danish cities of Roskilde and Kalundborg by a rail. It was now that his downfall began. Nobody would help him in his plan. To raise cash he sold unregistered stocks and bonds. He was arrested in 1878 and jailed for ten weeks. Thereafter, one disaster followed another. After his arrest, his wife left home and went to America. He never saw her again. His oldest son, Adolphe, who resided in Naples, committed suicide. As a result of his conviction, he lost his membership in the stock exchange. He tried to vindicate himself at all levels of the courts, up to the Danish Supreme Court, but always failed. Old, poor, and ill he died on March 10, 1892. At his funeral, only a few friends were present. He had travelled in the highest circles, but vanity and conceit had brought him low. As Professor Simonsen said at his funeral: "He was an example of earthly vanity . . . yet, to his last, his mind was still occupied with plans to help his poor co-religionists." A strange black, polished tombstone was placed on his grave. None of his children ever visited the grave.[35]

Emil Glückstadt, son of Isaak Glückstadt, who had been a Gedalia director at the Landmandsbanken, succeeded his father on that bank's board. Emil had received an extensive education in New

---

[34] Johannes Werner, *Gedalia og hans Forfaedre* (Copenhagen: H. Hirschprungs Forlag, 1933), p.85.
[35] *Ibid.*, p.216.

112 / The Viking Jews

York, London and Paris. His ambition was to make the Landmandsbanken an institution of international importance. When the bank celebrated its fiftieth anniversary, it was considered the biggest institution of its kind in Scandinavia.[36] However, its management was weak. Emil Glückstadt himself speculated in mines, which led to rumors being circulated that the bank was about to go bankrupt. Glückstadt was accused of fraud and imprisoned. During the court proceedings, he died. Although he was never vindicated, it was said of him that he remained faithful to his bank, his home, his family and friends. Above all, he remained a faithful member of the Jewish community, of which he was a leader for many years.[37]

The last quarter of the nineteenth century saw many Jews in positions of leadership in all fields. There were about twenty-five Jewish physicians, including Adolph Hannover (1814 - 1894) considered the grand old man of the Danish Medical Society. Dr. Harald Hirschprung (1830 - 1916) became a celebrated pediatrician at the Queen Louise Childrens' Hospital in Copenhagen.[38]

In the arts and literature, the painters David Monies (1812 - 1894) and Ernst Meyer (1797 - 1861) and the literary critic Paul Levin (1869 - 1929) were highly regarded. Henri Nathanson, the author, was known as the spokesman for Jewish conscience and Jewish nationalism.[39]

Michael Hartvig, in his book *Jøderne i Danmark* makes a most valid point when he says:

> The history of the Jews of Denmark is the record of how they grew together with the land. In numerous places they wove their threads into the fabric of the society, contributing to the culture of Denmark today. Many became tired in the constant battle against earlier prejudices . . . others lost contact with the Jewish people and assimilated themselves completely into Danish society. But most could not get themselves to bury the Jewish

---

[36] Borchsenius, p.193.
[37] Friediger, p.364.
[38] Borchsenius, p.205.
[39] Balsley, p.110.

past or deny Jewish ideals. They felt that the fate of the Jewish people also had a special message for them. These are the individuals which built and developed the Jewish community in Denmark.[40]

By the end of the century, the Jewish community of Copenhagen had become an established cohesive entity. When chief rabbi Wolff died in 1891, the kateket, David Jacob Simonsen, was elected in 1892 to take his place. He was the first chief rabbi born in Denmark. After holding that position for ten years, Simonsen resigned to dedicate himself entirely to Oriental studies.

Simonsen was born in 1853. He grew up in a truly orthodox home. As he himself stated: "My home was a Jewish home, not only in name, but in deed as well."[41] He made many contributions to the literary society *Mekize Nirdamim*, whose purpose was to reissue old manuscripts of literary or cultural-historic importance. His library, which he donated to the Royal Danish Library of Copenhagen, consisting of more than 40,000 books, became world famous. On his retirement he asked for and received the title of Professor rather than the Cross of the Order of Denmark, because he considered the former more in accord with his Jewish thinking.[42] On his seventieth birthday a *Festskrift* was issued, in which scholars from all over the world paid tribute to him.[43] For the rest of his life, he remained the unofficial leader of Denmark's Jews. He died in 1932.

---

[40] Michael Hartvig, *Jøderne i Danmark i Tiden 1600 – 1800* (Copenhagen: G. E. C. Gads Forlag, 1951), p.199.
[41] Friediger, p.358.
[42] Raphael Edelman, "David Simonsen," *Ved 150 Aars-Dagen for Anordningen af 29 Marts 1814* (Copenhagen : A/S Oscar Fraenkel & Co., 1964), p.111.
[43] *Festskrift i Anledning af Professor David Simonsen 70-aarige Fødselsdag* (Copenhagen: Hertz Bogtrykkeri, 1923).

IX

East European Immigration at the Turn of the Century

At the turn of the century, the Jewish community in Copenhagen was an integral part of the Danish middle class. Nearly all of its members were native born. The language they spoke was Danish. They were fully protected by the laws of the land. They were accepted in all social circles. They provided for their poorer brethren with numerous funds established within the Jewish community. There being no organized Conservative or Reform movements in Denmark, the community was basically united. All members could find their proper place within the established framework.

But this seeming peace and tranquility was fragile. Outside forces were impinging from various directions on the Jewish community. One of the strongest of these was assimilation. The goal of social, economic and political equality had been reached. The Jews spoke, dressed and behaved like other Danes. Interfaith marriages were on the rise. Between 1880 and 1905 there were 395 Jewish marriages and 272 interfaith marriages in the Jewish community. (40.7%). There were also conversions to Christianity, although no figures are available regarding baptism.[1] A journalist wrote in a Jewish weekly at the beginning of the twentieth century: "There is no danger that

---

[1] Benjamin Balslev, *De Danske Jøders Historie* (Copenhagen: O. Lohse, 1932), p.92.

a Jew might forget he is a Dane but many are on the way to forgetting that they are Jewish."[2]

Another force that exerted great pressure on the Jewish community was the appearance in Denmark of Polish and Russian Jewish refugees. The great mass of these unfortunates made their way to the United States, but enough of them settled in Copenhagen to create a problem for the shrinking Jewish community in Copenhagen. These new arrivals were completely different from the Danish Jews. The latter had gone far in the struggle for emancipation and were embarrassed in observing the peculiarly dressed Jewish individuals in the streets of Copenhagen. Not only their dress, but also their language, Yiddish, (which they called *mammeloshen*) and their behavior were quite different from what was considered the norm in the Jewish community of Copenhagen. By 1905, 264 of these mainly Polish and Russian Jews were residing in Copenhagen.[3] These individuals had come from an environment in which persecution was a nearly daily occurrence. They were unfamiliar with the liberal atmosphere of Denmark. Consequently, they all settled in close proximity of the synagogue, creating for the first time a "ghetto" in Copenhagen. This was, of course, a voluntary ghetto, formed by the new immigrants for their security.

The Danish Jewish community tried to help those who intended to move on to the United States to continue their journey. Those who decided to stay on in Denmark found a true friend in Professor Simonsen, who organized a special committee—*Russerkomite*—to help them. It was not long before Professor Simonsen's address became the best known and most used by any Jewish immigrant arriving in Copenhagen. Each one learned that Professor Simonsen never refused a Jew in need.[4] It is said, that now was the only time he regretted having resigned his position as chief rabbi. He gave every Jew that came to him moral, financial and spiritual assistance. All his energy was devoted to the *Russerkomite* which he chaired. The

---

[2] *Ibid.*
[3] *Ibid.*, p.102.
[4] Poul Borchsenius, *Historien om de danske Jøder* (København: Fremad, Det Hoffenbergske Establissement, 1969), p.243.

committee tried to help as many Jews as possible. Simonsen's deputy and co-worker was the physician, Dr. Louis Frankel (1868 - 1935), a Danish Jew who had not forgotten he was Jewish. Warmhearted, intelligent and understanding, Frankel towered above the entire community. His office was filled with "Russians" at all times. One evening when he returned home, he found no less than 76 immigrants in his apartment prepared to learn the Danish language.[5]

Dr. Frankel soon realized that his own quarters were inadequate to the demands being made upon them; so he established in Copenhagen the first "Toynbeehall" (named for the young English historian, Arnold Toynbee). In this "hall," which was actually another apartment, the Poles and Russians found a place to meet and continue to partake of the culture they had brought with them from the lands of their birth.[6]

The problems the immigrants presented were manifold. The Jewish community did not understand them. It could not comprehend what these unfortunate individuals had experienced in Russia and Poland. And the immigrants were far removed from the interests and attitudes of the Danish Jews. Indeed, they seemed to have no intention of relinquishing their Yiddish language, their culture or their heritage. They founded their own organizations, to serve the various needs of their youth in sports, work and education.[7]

Thus at the dawn of the twentieth century, the Jews of Denmark were composed of two distinct groups: the old assimilated families – Viking-Jews, as they liked to call themselves – and on the other, the new immigrants, who were unable to communicate with them. Some years had to pass before a new, authentic synthesis could be fashioned between them. Yet it was ultimately these new immigrants who saved the Jewish community from disintegration. Later becoming prominent, loyal and devoted members of the community, they gave it a new lease on life, assuring the continuation of the long and

---

[5] Julius Margolinsky (ed.), *Danmarks Loge, U. O. B. B. No. 712* (København: A/S Oscar Fraenkel & Co., 1962), p.21.
[6] *Ibid.*
[7] *Ibid.*, p.22.

proud history of Danish Jewry. As Hillel Nakman says of these new immigrants: "It was good that such a rich cultural life was found in Copenhagen. Poor, indeed, would the picture have been, if this would not have been the case."[8] As the years went on, this unique, small but active entity became a creative force in the Jewish community, permitting it to look towards the future with optimism and assurance.

---

[8] Hillel Nakman, "Et lille jødisk Tidsbillede fra Haveforeningerne 'Taga' og 'Liljen'," *Ved 150 Aars-Dagen for Anordningen af 29 Marts, 1814*, ed. Julius Margolinsky og Poul Meyer (København: A/S Oscar Fraenkel & Co., 1964), p.220.

X

German Immigration To Denmark

In the spring of 1933 the sun was rapidly setting on German Jewry. The virus of Nazism had seriously infected Denmark's southerly neighbor. Social, economic and cultural discrimination against German Jews had become widespread; laws restricting their liberties began to be proclaimed.

Yet in Denmark there was no fear. An atmosphere of confidence, security and warmth filled the synagogue in Krystalgade, as, on April 21, 1933, the Jewish community celebrated the one hundredth anniversary of its dedication. This celebration was an event marked by grandeur, humility and prayers. King Christian X, who would later play an important role in the lives of Jews during the German occupation attended the services. His visit on this occasion laid the foundation of understanding between the Danish monarchy and Danish Jewry which would prove so important in the trying years Denmark was later to experience. A memento of that memorable day of the king's visit to the synagogue has been inscribed on the womens' balcony in golden letters. It reads: "The one hundredth anniversary of the dedication of the synagogue was celebrated in the presence of King Christian the Tenth, in the twenty-first year of his reign."[1]

---

[1] Friediger, p.360.

It is important to realize, in considering the immigration to Denmark after 1933, that Denmark had laws concerning entrance, permanent residence and work requirements for foreigners. Such laws had been enacted in all European countries. The Danish laws, however, were in no wise aimed at the Jews; they were primarily intended to combat unemployment among the native population. The financial crisis in the United States had sent repercussions throughout the world, including Denmark, and the government had set certain guide lines to govern the entrance of new people into the country.[2] Basic to these rules was the principle that only individuals who had some "association or connection" to Denmark could obtain an entrance permit. This permit was valid for six months, after which it had to be renewed by the State police.[3]

Meant by "association or connection" was the citizenship of a parent or of a close relative either born in Denmark or naturalized there. But the term was interpreted liberally. For instance, the present writer's grandmother was born in Copenhagen in 1850, was married and moved to Germany in 1868, lived in Germany for more than seventy years, and was permitted to return to Denmark as a ninety-year-old lady. She had "Association" to Denmark. Similarly, a number of her children, born and raised in Germany together with their foreign-born marriage partners, were able to obtain entrance permits on the basis of this "connection." Once in Denmark, they were able to stay permanently, and after the required time became Danish citizens.

However, immigrants without "association or connection" who had a visa to a foreign country, or could prove that a visa would be issued to them within a short time, could obtain a transit visa to Denmark. But these people were seldom granted permission to work. And so, when the first Jewish immigrants arrived in Denmark from Germany with horror stories of their personal experiences, the Jewish community acknowledged its responsibilities and organized a committee to assist them. It was given the neutral name of the Committee of May 4, 1933.[4]

---

[2] Det Mosaiske Troessamfund, p.206.
[3] German passport # 496.
[4] Danmark Loge, p.64.

This was not, of course, the first time that the Jewish community had formed a committee to deal with Jewish refugees. Thirty years earlier, a similar committee had been formed to aid East European refugees under the leadership of Professor David Simonsen. Simonsen had died on June 15, 1932. But Josef Fischer, dayan of the Jewish community, who had worked with him, joined the newly established Committee of May 4, 1933.

Once the earlier committee had solved the basic problems of the East European refugees, it had directed its efforts towards social and cultural ends. Thus, the Denmark Lodge of B'nai B'rith established a Subcommittee of February 7, 1922, whose prime purpose was to come in contact with the Russian and Polish Jews living in Denmark in order to enhance and further their "culture." Five branches of the subcommittee were set up to work on particular tasks: language education; lectures for men and women about Danish history, geography and culture; home visitations; and "to follow and assist the young men and women after they had left the schools."[5]

Thus, the Committee of May 4, 1933 had a certain amount of past experience and knowledge to guide it. When the German refugees started to arrive, the committee went into immediate action to provide bare economic necessities for these unfortunate individuals. A public kosher kitchen was established in Ny Kongensgade, in the Jewish community center, where the refugees could eat their main meal gratis. This kosher kitchen was sponsored and maintained by the Jewish community until October, 1943. With the financial help of the Joint Distribution Committee and other world Jewish organizations, it became possible to send some of the immigrants to other countries.

The only provisional stay and temporary working permits obtained were for the approximately 1,500 *chaluzim* who came to Denmark from 1933 until the beginning of World War II. It was understood that these immigrants had come to Denmark for preparation to go to Palestine.

It is estimated that about 4,500 Jewish refugees came to Denmark from spring, 1933, until April 9, 1940, when the country was occu-

---

[5] *Ibid.*, p.51.

pied by Germany. At that time 3,000 had already left Denmark again, among them approximately 1,000 *chaluzim*, who had stayed between one year and eighteenth months.[6]

Another perspective on immigration of this period can be obtained by analyzing the data gathered in Stockholm in the spring of 1945 by Julius Margolinsky.[7] A total of 795 men and 580 women (Jewish and "half-Jewish" immigrants) were registered at the refugee office in Stockholm as coming from Denmark and staying in Sweden from October, 1943, to May, 1945. These 1,375 immigrants had come to Denmark after 1933.

It is important to remember that no immigrant entered Denmark after the German occupation on April 9, 1940. In general, the non-Danish citizens that fled to Sweden in October, 1943, can be divided into four groups:

Jewish immigrants and others of Jewish descent who immigrated to Denmark after 1933;

Russian and East European Jews and their minor children who had lived in Denmark for some years but had not obtained Danish citizenship;

persons born in Sweden but married to Danish citizens, who together with their children, became naturalized as Swedish citizens; and

non-Jewish immigrants.

The non-Danish immigrants who came to Sweden claimed their birthplace as follows:

Germany	995
Austria	126
Czechoslovakia	102
Hungary	23
Russia, Poland, etc.	369
Sweden	101

---

[6] *Det Mosaiske Troessamfund*, p.207.

[7] Julius Margolinsky, *Statistiske Undersøgelser over Fordelingen paa Alder og Køn m.m. blandt Flygtninge fra Danmark i Sverige* (Stockholm, 1945), Copy #71, p.9.

Other countries	91
Denmark	280
Total	2087

According to sex and age, the group broke down as follows:

Men		1083
Women		655
Children under 18 years		
born in: Denmark	222	
Sweden	59	
Other countries	68	349
Total		2087

With regard to residence and birth in Denmark:

Residing in Denmark before 1933	411
Arrived in Denmark after 1933	1264
Arrival time unknown	73
	1748
Born in Denmark (from non-Danish parents)	280
Born in Sweden	59
Total	2087

These figures only take into consideration the citizenship of the immigrants and their arrival date in Denmark. One point which must be remembered is that a number of the registered women had in the meantime married and obtained Danish citizenship.

Of the total of 1,375 Jewish and "half-Jewish" immigrants, including 195 children, in Sweden, approximately 200 were women who had either married Danish citizens or were divorced from Danish citizens. Thus, a total of 1,176 of the Jewish immigrants in Sweden were stateless. About 100 of the children were born in Denmark, 49 in Sweden, and 46 in other countries.

The number of East European Jews who had previously immigrated and who were not Danish citizens, including their children, was about 540. This group consisted of 380 adults, 160 minors, of which 140 were born in Denmark or Sweden.

The number of non-Jewish immigrants from Central Europe and other non-Danish citizens who came to Sweden amounted to about 300 persons.

We shall now turn our attention to the *chaluzim* who comprised the largest group of individuals to enter Denmark in the period 1933 – 1940. A detailed account of the *chaluz* program in Scandinavia is given by Professor Hugo Valentin of Uppsala, Sweden, in his report *Rescue and Relief Activities in Behalf of Jewish Victims of Nazism in Scandinavia* (YIVO Annual of Social Science, Vol. VIII, N.Y. 1953/54).

Because of the liberal social and cultural situation in Denmark, Zionistic feelings among Danish Jews did not run high. The old Danish Jewish families – "Viking Jews" – focused their attention on the synagogue in Krystalgade and the various organizations engaged in cultural and humanitarian activities. The East European Jews who had arrived about 1903 – 1904 were to a greater or lesser extent associated with the Bund. They were either hostile towards Zionism or remained indifferent to it.

It was not until Benjamin Slor arrived in Copenhagen in 1913 that the word and the political idea of Zionism began to circulate in Denmark. Slor had come to Denmark to receive an education. His aim was to become a physical training instructor in Palestine. He was born in 1892 in Petach Tikva. The outbreak of the First World War prevented his return to Palestine, and so he stayed on to launch the Zionist movement in Denmark.

Because of his connection with the folk high schools in which he received his education, Slor was able to make contact with farmers' associations. Through the Agricultural-Economic Travel Agency, a semi-official government bureau which arranged exchanges of agriculture students with other countries, he managed to bring *chaluzim* to Danish farms and dairy factories. These students were to receive instruction in agriculture which they could later use in Palestine. The *chaluzim* received no wages from the farmers; only food, lodging and a little spending money. Before 1933 there had been only 15 *chaluzim* in Denmark. No permanent organization to aid them existed, as no further expansion in their numbers was envisioned.[8]

[8] Julius Margolinsky, "The German Hecalutz in Denmark" (unpublished), p.4.

In the summer of 1933, as outside pressure increased, the Committee of May 4, 1933 planned to apply to the government to grant permission for twenty *chaluzim* to enter individually from Germany. This request was granted. But the situation in Germany deteriorated rapidly, and it became clear that more *chaluzim* had to be brought to safety. By September, 1933, a total of one hundred and twenty *chaluzim* (92 males, 28 females) had entered Denmark. In the following years the number varied between 200 and 250. After *Krystallnacht* (the night between November 9-10, 1938, when all synagogues were destroyed in Germany) the Committee applied to the government for 500 entrance permits. Although the government acted swiftly and sympathetically to grant the request, not all of the entrance permits were used, as some *chaluzim* had obtained visas to other countries. Originally only German *chaluzim* had entered Denmark, but after the Anschluss of Austria and the invasion of Czechoslovakia, 150 *chaluzim* were admitted from Vienna and Prague.[9]

These *chaluzim* were stationed in rural areas of the country. Rarely did they come to Copenhagen. But the Copenhagen Jews soon became curious about these youngsters scattered about in Danish villages and hamlets. The words "certificate" and "affidavit" were spoken by more and more people, some of whom had no conception of their meaning. But they knew that the young men and women working on farms in the country all waiting for the Certificates, and that other immigrants were daily expecting the affidavits. In fact, certificates were the official British documents which gave permission to enter Palestine, and the affidavits were the Affidavit of Support required by any immigrant hoping to enter the United States. In the first few years, the *chaluzim* came to Copenhagen to celebrate the High Holidays and were lodged in the homes of local Jewish families. Later, they seemed to prefer to observe the holidays together in their own communities. Two of such communities were situated in Saunte and Smidstrup near Elsinore.

At the time the Second World War started, about 1,000 *chaluzim* had departed from Denmark. Of these, approximately 600 arrived in Palestine; about 350 continued their agricultural education in

[9] *Ibid.*

other lands and about 50 emigrated to the United States.[10]

The plans and dreams of these young men and women were shattered on April 9, 1940, when Germany occupied Denmark. Their insecurity about themselves and their closest relatives coupled with the prospect that they might never reach Palestine prompted a few to embark on desperate actions. A group of *chaluzim*, unnoticed, entered a German freight train in Denmark which was destined for Balkan countries. They were discovered at the border and sent to concentration camps, where they perished.[11]

Ten *chaluzim* had better luck when, in April 1943, they took possession of a boat on the Danish island of Bornholm and escaped to neutral Sweden. But they had been observed by the Germans. Through the Danish Justice Department the Jewish community was informed that any such action in the future would have the most serious consequences for Danish Jewry. The Secretariat – as the Committee of May, 1933 now was called – had to demand of the *chaluzim* that they refrain from such behavior in the future. As is well known – and will be discussed later – this request was heeded for only six months. By October, 1943, most Jews were in process of escaping to Sweden.

As of September 29, 1943 (when the Germans began their persecution of Danish Jews) a total of 360 adults and 29 children were registered with the Secretariat. Of these, 329 adults and 26 children were able to reach Sweden. Twenty-eight adults and 3 children were deported to Theresienstadt, where one girl who had been sick in Denmark died. Three *chaluzim* drowned crossing the Øresund to Sweden.[12]

At this point mention must be made of the Youth Aliyah, which first started in the summer of 1939. As the *chaluzim* worked through a semi-official travel-agency, the Youth Aliyah had its own administration, the International Women's League for Peace and Freedom, which represented the children to the various government agencies. Daily work was conducted, however, by a special commit-

[10] *Ibid.*, p.5.
[11] *Ibid.*, p.7.
[12] *Ibid.*, p.8.

tee consisting of members of the *chaluz* movement, a *madrich* from Palestine, and a few women of the Jewish community.[13]

A total of 174 *Ligabørn* (League children), as they came to be known, were in Denmark during the time of the occupation. Tragically, 40 of these young children were deported to Theresienstadt. The rest escaped to Sweden. Upon arrival there, they were integrated together with the *chaluzim* from Denmark into the Swedish *chaluz* program.[14]

To obtain a total picture of the immigration to Denmark it is important to recall that after April 9, 1940, no more immigrants arrived in Denmark. Those immigrants who became stranded in Denmark had to adjust to new conditions with the prospect of remaining until the conclusion of the war. Thus, foreign Jews were present in the country until October, 1943. When the Germans began their raids upon the Jews, they were successful in arresting and deporting a total of 464 persons to Theresienstadt. The following table represents a breakdown, according to group, of these deported Jews.

Table 18[15]

	Deported to Theresienstadt		total	Settled in Sweden	total
	Men	Women			
Old Danish-Jewish families. (Group I)					
Under 18 years	5	2	7	121	128
18 – 34 years	19	7	26	252	278
35 – 59 years	13	27	40	632	672
60 years and over	22	35	57	426	483
Total	59	71	130	1431	1561
East-European Jews (Group II)					
Under 18 years	18	21	39	521	560
18 – 34 years	29	32	61	1134	1195

---

[13] *Ibid.*, p.5.
[14] *Ibid.*, p.8.
[15] *Statistiske Undersøgelser*, p.12.

35 – 59 years	44	37	81	1093	1174
60 years and over	24	23	47	364	411
Total	115	113	228	3112	3340

German–Jewish Immigrants (Group III)

Under 18 years	4	3	7	134	141
18 – 34 years	48	21	69	520	589
35 – 59 years	11	5	16	487	503
60 years and over	6	8	14	128	142
Total	69	37	106	1269	1375

Summary

	Deported to Theresienstadt	In Sweden	Total
Group I	130	1431	1561
Group II	228	3112	3340
Group III	106	1269	1375
	464	5812	6276

Besides the 464 persons who were deported to Theresienstadt, three were deported to other concentration camps. Five were returned to Denmark from Theresienstadt some time after the deportation.

Died in Theresienstadt:	Group I	31 persons
	Group II	15 "
	Group III	2 "
	Total	48 persons
Born in Theresienstadt:	Group III	2 "
Liberated from Theresienstadt:		
Deported persons + newborn		418 persons
Persons with Danish "connections"		7 "
Total liberated Jews from Denmark:		425 persons

As mentioned earlier, a total of about 1,269 persons who had immigrated to Denmark after 1933 arrived in Sweden in October,

1943. Of this group (III) 106 were deported to Theresienstadt; of these persons, the largest number (69) were between the ages of 18 and 34. They were all either League children (40) or *chaluzim* (29).

These numbers may seem small compared to the total Jewish population of Europe. Yet, one must not minimize the fact that Denmark, bordering on Germany, provided many with a difficult choice of residence. Also, the total number of "foreigners" residing in Denmark on April 9, 1940, including *chaluzim* and League children, was close to 20% of the total Jewish population in the country. One more point must still be made. After April 9, 1940, every Jew in Denmark, regardless of national origin, was considered "Danish". By then all had some "association or connection." This is proven by the well-known facts that, even during the imprisonment in Theresienstadt, *all* were treated by the Germans as Danes, *all* were visited and acknowledged by the Danish committee which inspected this "model" concentration camp in 1944, and *all* who survived returned to Denmark in spring, 1945. Denmark clearly, was a country which realized its responsibilities and made every effort to assure that all who had lived within its borders received every benefit the country was able to provide during the most trying years in its long history.

Chief Rabbi Dr. M. Friediger (1884–1947) ministered to the Jewish community from 1921–1947. From October 1943 to April 1945 he was in the German concentration camp Theresienstadt.
Courtesy Arne and Helene Meyer

XI

The Occupation

On a beautiful Tuesday morning, April 9, 1940, Copenhagen awoke to a strange noise. Airplanes were flying over the city. Soon the streets were littered with green leaflets announcing that Germany had assumed the "protection" of Denmark. The people were shocked. This writer, going to school, remembers how they looked, asking each other if war had really come to Denmark. Within a few hours German soldiers were standing guard at all important buildings. All major roads were controlled by the Wehrmacht. The occupation of Denmark had been swift and thorough.[1]

The green leaflets contained a lengthy proclamation from the German commander in chief, Kaupisch, to the Danish people. It was written in a pathetic mixture of Danish and Norwegian, with garbled syntax and peculiar diction and spelling.* But its essential message was crystal clear. In the afternoon, people hurried home carrying rolls of black paper to darken their windows. Towards evening, Copenhagen and the rest of the country were completely dark. The gay, bright capital had become a dark ghost city. What the future would bring nobody knew.

---

[1] A detailed description of the occupation of Denmark is found in *The Rise and Fall of the Third Reich* by William L. Shirer. pp. 694 - 700. See also in *Yad Voshem*: Olaf Abitz, *Livres danois sur l'occupation*, Aarhus Statsbiblioteket, #801, p. 10.
*See Appendix III, p. 154.

One sentence in the German proclamation gave the Danish Jews reason to hope for their survival. It said: "that the Danish kingdom shall continue to exist, that the fleet shall be maintained, that the liberty of the Danish people shall be respected, and that the future independence of the country shall be secured."[2] During the morning hours of April 9th, all over the city big white posters started to appear. They contained a proclamation to the Danish people signed by Prime Minister Stauning.

> To the Danish people!
> German troops last night crossed the Danish frontier and have landed in various places. The Danish Government has decided under protest to arrange the affairs of the country with a view to the occupation which has taken place, in pursuance whereof the following announcement is made: The German troops which are now present in the country have entered into contact with the Danish Defence Force, and it is the duty of the population to refrain from any resistance to these troops. The Danish Government will endeavor to safeguard the Danish people and our country against the disaster resulting from war conditions and therefore urges the population to adopt a calm and restrained attitude to the conditions which have now arisen. Quiet and order must prevail in the country and a loyal attitude must be displayed to all who have authority to exercise.

To these words the king had added words of his own: "Under the present conditions, which are so momentous for our fatherland, I beg you all in town and country to maintain perfectly correct and dignified behavior, remembering that any ill-considered deed or word may entail the gravest consequences. God keep you all! God keep Denmark!"[3]

From accounts given at Nuremberg and at the Eichmann trial, it is clear that the occupation of Denmark was well planned and executed. From the very beginning, the relationship between Denmark and Germany was on a somewhat different level than that of

---

[2] Raphael Lemkin, *Axis Rule in Occupied Europe* (New York, Columbia University Press, 1944), pp. 377 - 378.
[3] *Ibid.*, p.158.

any other country occupied by Germany. The Danish population adhered minutely to the requests of the king and prime minister.

The acceptance of the German troops by the Danish population, and the cooperation between the Danish government and the German military forces clearly affected the status of Danish Jews. As Harold Flender in his book *Rescue in Denmark* says correctly: "The Danes had been friendly to the Germans, and in appreciation the Germans were considerate to the Danes. Christian X was permitted to remain head of state, the Danish parliament and Danish courts were allowed to function, the Nuremberg edicts against Jews were not introduced in Denmark."[4] Furthermore, in other countries which Germany occupied, it tried to instigate its racial theories and practices among the native population. In Poland, Slovakia and the Ukraine, particularly, the program met with horrendous success. Denmark was spared this horror.

Flender makes the point that "Hitler had a soft spot in his heart for Denmark: he considered the Danes pure Nordics, since they were descended from the same stock who had inhabited the Danish islands from before the Stone Age. The Kimbric peninsula, Jutland, was the birthplace of the Teutons and the Gottons, and the Danes were blood brothers to the Germans, according to Nazi philosophy."[5] Anything that disturbed the special relationship between Germany and Denmark was of no advantage to either side; and the Germans soon realized that introduction of the Nuremberg laws would, indeed, upset the equlibrium. They would meet stiff opposition from the Danes if they promulgated anti-Jewish edicts. So the Jews had "peace" until 1943.

Laws which were introduced by the Germans had nothing specifically to do with the Jews. Through the Danish government, laws were passed regarding the importation and exportation of money and securities, communistic activities, the forced selling of food and dairy products to Germany, and so forth. Besides these laws, there were also the usual military regulations and prohibitions relat-

---

[4] Harold Flender, *Rescue in Denmark*, (Macfadden-Bartell Co. New York, 1963), p.24.
[5] *Ibid.*

ing to radio transmission, photography of German military installations, private firearms and the like.[6] Most of these laws and regulations had little effect on the general public. Thus, a few days after April 9, 1940, most Danish citizens, including Jews, were back at their usual jobs.

The Danes had taken the German proclamation of April 9, 1940, at face value. In it, the German military commander had promised that there would be no interference in the internal affairs of Denmark. Everybody, including the Jews, relied on this promise. There was widespread belief that nothing drastic would happen as long as Christian X was king, a Danish government existed, Danish law courts functioned, and Danish police patrolled the streets. In this connection, it must be mentioned that the morale of Danish citizens was greatly bolstered when they saw the king riding daily unescorted through the most populated area of Copenhagen. It was quite common to see the king stop and shake hands with some of his subjects. The Germans could not comprehend a king without military or police escort riding through the city streets. Asked who guards the king, Danes would answer: "There are more than one million human hearts in Copenhagen that watch over the king. He has nothing to fear!"

Numerous stories have been told about the king's threat to wear the yellow Star of David if the Jews were forced to do so. There seems to be no truth to these stories, some of which depict the king actually wearing the star. This writer had many opportunities to observe the king riding through the streets of Copenhagen and never saw the king so adorned. A detailed study of the stories and their basis was done a number of years ago by Jens Lund,[7] who was forced to conclude: "The allegation of the king's threat (to wear the yellow star) eventually became a legend of the king's act, and ultimately of the Danish people's act. All of the complex events surrounding the rescue of the Danish Jews by a cooperating group of Danes, Swedes and Germans are thus made metaphor in the legend of the

---

[6] R. Lemkin, pp.378 - 379.

[7] Jens Lund, *Indiana Folklore*, Vol VII, Number 1-2, Indiana University Research Center, Bloomington, Indiana, 1975.

King and the Star."[8] The imaginative character of the stories is also attested to by the Danish historians Per Haestrup and Ole Barfoed, leading authorities on this period, as well as by others. Furthermore, Nuremberg trial (NG-5121) and Eichmann trial (T 580) documents establish that the German Foreign Ministry rejected the introduction of the Nuremberg decrees, including the wearing of the yellow star, in Denmark. Nevertheless, that King Christian X was implacably opposed to anti-Semitism is firmly established.

The internal Jewish community life continued as previously. Religious services were conducted in the main synagogue in Krystalgade, in the *Machazekay Hadass* as well as in the synagogue in Laederstraede.

Daily services, mornings and evenings, as well as Sabbath and holiday services, were held in all the three above mentioned synagogues throughout the German occupation.

The two Jewish newspapers *Jødisk Samfund* and *Jødisk Familieblad* did not appear anymore. Otherwise, all other Jewish societies, organizations and religious institutions continued to exist and function without interference, though in somewhat curtailed form. However, Jewish butcher stores removed the three Hebrew letters spelling Kosher from their windows.

In 1941 two books on Jewish subjects appeared in Danish. One, written by Rabbis Wolf S. Jacobson (of the *Machazekay Hadass*) and Marcus Melchior (Principal of the Jewish School), was called *Glimt af Jødedommen* (A Glimmer of Judaism) and dealt with interpretation of the weekly Torah reading. In the preface, Rabbi Jacobson stated that when the human being is in need, the soul searches for the calming words of the Bible. The book was sold openly and many bookstores displayed copies in the windows. After the flight to Sweden, Jacobson's co-author, Dr. Melchior, became rabbi of the Danish Jews in Sweden. Chief Rabbi Max Friediger, who was transported to Theresienstadt, returned to Denmark after the war and resumed his position as rabbi until his death in 1947, when Melchior succeeded him.

---

[8] *Ibid.*, p.30.

The other book referred to was *Almenmenneskelige Vaerdier* (All Human Values) by Rudolph Simonsen. It dealt with three spiritual giants, Plato, Spinoza and Goethe. In his preface the author spoke of difficult times in which people are freezing and need the warmth that radiates from human values tested over hundreds of years. This book was also sold publicly and it was well received by reviewers in the daily press.

In the summer of 1942, over 1,200 gift parcels were sent from Denmark to Jews in Poland, Germany, Holland and France. The value of these parcels is estimated as close to 30,000 Danish kroner. In addition, small packets containing cheese, imitation honey, tea and sugar were sent by individual Jews to friends and relatives in the Theresienstadt concentration camp. Some of these packets did arrive at their intended destination, for occasionally a post card with the signature of the recipient would be received in Copenhagen.

The vast majority of Danes were strongly opposed to anti-Semitism in any form. The tiny minority of Danish Nazis could not make headway. Their weekly newspaper *Faedrelandet*, moulded after the German *Der Stürmer*, was primarily bought by Jews curious to see whose face graced the current front page. It ceased publication shortly after it began to appear for lack of subscribers.

In 1941 an attempt was made by Germans to set the synagogue in Krystalgade on fire. The attempt was thwarted by the quick action of Danish police. A year later in December, 1942, a similar attempt was made and failed again. The only damage the Germans were able to do was to paint swastikas on the synagogue walls. Consequently, the Danish police formed a special unit of Jewish youths to watch the synagogue. The young men were armed with clubs and guns. An electric warning system was installed, linking the synagogue with Danish police headquarters. Cots were placed in a building adjacent to the synagogue on which the guards could wait and rest. No further disturbances occurred. After the first incident in 1941, the king sent a personal letter, dated December 31, 1941, to Chief Rabbi Friediger in which he said: "I have heard about the attempted fire at the synagogue, and I am very happy that there was only slight damage. I beg of you to give my congratulations and best wishes for the New Year to your congregation."

The 100th anniversary of Georg Brandes' birth was celebrated in Copenhagen on February 4, 1942. In the Students' Organization of Copenhagen's university a special lecture was held. Hartvig Frisch spoke about Georg Brandes, his life and work. The hall was packed to capacity and many prominent Danes attended this lecture. There was no disturbance or disorder.[9]

The Denmark Lodge of B'nai B'rith also held a number of lectures devoted to various subjects. In one, which took place in 1941, the director for the Glyptotek, Dr. F. Poulsen, spoke about Semitic Places of Culture in Syria and Palestine.[10]

Such sufferings and inconveniences as the Jews underwent they shared with the rest of the Danish population: darkened windows, shortages of certain foods, having to listen to and read German-controlled radios and newspapers, and the constant sight of foreign soldiers. But as the summer of 1943 came to a close, a new situation arose in Denmark which would place the Jews in a most precarious situation. Still, the Danes did not forget their humanitarian traditions, and the actions they took to save their Jewish fellow citizens were unique to any country occupied by the German war machine.

---

[9] Letter from Julius Margolinsky. In Hartvig Frisch's book *Taenkt og talt under Krigen*, p.27 the speech is also mentioned. In his other book *Danmark besat og befriet*, the anniversary of Georg Brandes and the lecture at the Studenterforeningen is also discussed in detail

[10] Danmark Loge 1962, p.75. The Glyptotek is a Copenhagen museum of Oriental art.

Rabbi Wolf S. Jacobson (1894-1973) ministered to the Machazike Hadass Congregation from 1933-1943.
Courtesy Rabbi B. Borchardt

XII

October, 1943

In the summer of 1943 the tide of the World War began to turn. The German armies were in rapid retreat on the eastern front. The nightly bombing of German cities by the Allied air forces damaged the productive capacity and shattered the morale of the German heartland itself. Everybody began to see the final outcome of the war.

Sabotage and other acts of destruction against its war machine occurred daily in all the countries occupied by Germany. In Denmark, where sabotage at the beginning of the war had rarely occurred, a sudden increase in such activities became noticeable. In mid-summer of 1943, they seemed to be taking place everywhere in Denmark that Germans lived. Factories producing goods for Germany were destroyed. Railroad tracks were put out of service. Ships connecting the various islands of Denmark were halted. The entire transportation system seemed to come to a halt. The German ambassador, Dr. Werner Best, made an official request of the Danish government that in the future saboteurs be tried by German military courts.[1] The administration of justice in Denmark under German occupation had been the subject of numerous negotiations between the German occupation force and the Danish government. The basic question of which laws and courts – Danish or German –

---

[1] Lemkin, p.164.

should have authority over Danish citizens accused of sabotage and other crimes against the German army was with few exceptions settled in favor of the former.² The Danish government did not accept Dr. Best's request and threatened to resign if he pressed it further. The Danish population applauded the government's response, and immediately anti-German activities increased. Then neutral Sweden, which had permitted German troops to use Swedish railroads to reach destinations in occupied Norway, withdrew its permission on August 5, 1943. No longer would Sweden allow German troops to pass through their country.³ This action inspired Danish dock workers at Odense, on the island of Fyen, to go on strike. They refused to repair or load any German ships. There were riots, and arrests were made by the Germans. On August 9, 1943, the Danish prime minister threatened to resign with his entire government if the Danish courts were forced to try the arrested men. Consequently, martial law was declared in Odense.[4]

On August 24, l943, the Danish resistance movement blew up the German-occupied Forum hall in Copenhagen, and on the following day all Danish shipyards went on strike. On August 28th, Danish Prime Minister Scavenius and the whole cabinet resigned. Sunday morning, August 29th, German General von Hannecken, commander of all German forces in Denmark, proclaimed martial law throughout Denmark. The Danish government was interned, and the king was made prisoner in his summer castle, Sorgenfri, near Lyngby. The Danish cabinet was dismissed and parliament dissolved.[5] The daily management of the country was placed in the hands of the individual government departments on the instigation and with the approval of the king. When the Germans tried to take over the Danish navy, however, part of it was scuttled by Danish patriots and part of it escaped to Sweden.[6] Werner Best, the Ger-

[2] *Ibid.*, p.163.
[3] Gerald Reitlinger, *The Final Solution* (London: Vallentine, Mitchell & Co., 1953), p.345.
[4] *Ibid.*, p.346.
[5] Bertelsen, pp.10–11.
[6] Lemkin, p.164

man ambassador, became the highest authority in Denmark.[7]

On the same day, August 29th, a number of prominent Danish citizens were arrested. Among them were also some Jews; Chief Rabbi Friediger, the president of the Jewish community, C. B. Henriques, and the chairman of the synagogue committee. Henriques, however, was soon released. The prisoners were first brought to the public school in Copenhagen. Later they were transferred to the Horserød camp, where the Germans had previously imprisoned all Danish Communists.[8]

The Jewish community in Copenhagen viewed the entire situation with great concern. On September 17th the Gestapo made a thorough search of the offices of the Jewish community in Ny Kongensgade. They removed lists containing the names of Danish Jews as well as other documents. The Jewish community had no idea of what the Germans' act portended. Inquiries were made by prominent Jews to those Danish authorities they believed could provide some clues of German intentions, but without success. The Jewish community lived in suspense and uncertainty from August 29th on.[9]

From all available sources, it is clear that the conditions which now prevailed in Denmark were to no one's liking. The German ambassador, Dr. Best, found himself impaled on the horns of a dilemma. Hitler and Himmler were now demanding the "final solution" of Danish Jewry. This could only be effected while martial law prevailed throughout the country. However, Dr. Best realized that a campaign against the Jews would only increase Danish resistance and preferred to have nothing to do with it. A special group of Gestapo commandos from Eichmann's office in Berlin arrived in Copenhagen on September 18th. Thus an internal German fight began over who should carry out the destruction of Danish Jewry. The Wehrmacht (German army) sidestepped the issue, claiming it was a political and not a military problem. According to

---

[7] Yad Voshem: *Best-Sagen*, Københavns Byret, Øster landsret, og Højsteretsdomme, C.E.Gad, 1950 (64 pages).
[8] Danmark Loge, p.76.
[9] *Ibid.*

Carl Bertil Henriques (1870–1957) served as president of the Jewish community during the German occupation of Denmark.
Courtesy Arne and Helene Meyer

142 / The Viking Jews

Gerald Reitlinger, "The truth would seem to be that Werner Best, in company with the German commander von Hennecken and even the local German Security Police chief were seized at the last moment with fear of the world publicity which this action by Himmler must entail."[10]

The first phase of the "action against the Jews" had to be initiated by the Gestapo. It planned the arrests of all Danish Jews on the night between October 1st and 2nd. After this initial phase was completed the Jews would be transported to German concentration camps by ship. For this purpose Werner Best informed the German director of his shipping operation in Denmark, Georg F. Duckwitz, on September 18th, that a number of German transport ships would anchor in Copenhagen's harbor ten days later. These vessels would be used to transport the Jews to the concentration camps.

On September 25th, Duckwitz, on his own initiative, flew to Stockholm and pleaded with the Swedish prime minister to accept the Danish Jews. Sweden agreed to receive them, provided that Germany approved. Duckwitz would be informed of Berlin's answer in Copenhagen by the Swedish envoy residing in Copenhagen. Duckwitz thereupon flew back to Copenhagen.

For two days Duckwitz waited to hear from Sweden's envoy. When no word came, he went secretly to a meeting of a committee of the Danish Socialist Democrats, on Tuesday afternoon, September 28th, and revealed the German plan for Danish Jewry. He even told the committee the time of the "action against the Jews": the night of October 1st. Present at the meeting were Hans Hedtoft, later Danish prime minister, Vilhelm Buhl, H.C. Hansen and Herman Dedichen, all prominent political figures. When Duckwitz had left, these four immediately called for Danish secret police automobiles and visited as many Jewish friends as possible. The word spread rapidly throughout the Jewish community. The following morning, it was announced in the synagogue in Krystalgade. The people were strongly advised not to stay home any longer, but to get away, and if possible to Sweden. Most Jews heeded the advice, and when the Gestapo raids took place Rosh Hashono night

[10] Reitlinger, p.347.

most German commandos returned to their barracks empty handed. Only 464 Jews were arrested. The rest, close to 6,000, were not at home.[11]

Was it possible that the 464 arrested Jews did not receive warning in time? This is doubtful. Perhaps a few who lived far away from the city did not hear about the forthcoming raids. But to the rest the likelihood seemed far fetched. Germany had been in Demark for three and one-half years. Why should they start to persecute Jews now? Impossible! Others felt that they were too old (25% of those arrested were 60 years and older) for the Germans to be interested in them. Still others, unfortunately, had no place where to go. To a large degree, this group comprised the League Children.

When the Germans realized on the morning of October 2nd that the operation had been a fiasco, they read the following proclamation over the radio and published it in the newspapers:

> Since the Jews, who, with their anti-German provocation and their moral and material support to terrorism and sabotage, to a considerable extent contributed to the aggravated situation in Denmark, and since, thanks to the precautions taken by the Germans, these Jews have been secluded from public life and prevented from poisoning the atmosphere, the German command will, in order to fulfill the wishes cherished by most of the Danish people, begin to release within the next few days interned Danish soldiers, and this release will continue at a pace decided by the technical possibilities.[12]

The Germans hoped to get the Danes to reveal the hiding places of the Jews, assuming they would readily betray them to hasten the release of imprisoned Danish troops. But not even this treacherous trick worked.

Illegal Danish newspapers, distributed all over the city of Copenhagen, condemned the Germans for their inhuman actions. On Oc-

---

[11] In this connection, it should be mentioned that Georg F. Duckwitz became the first ambassador from West Germany to Denmark after the war. His humane behavior during the war had made him acceptable to all Danes.
[12] Flender, P.57

Moses Bamberger (1886–1962) served as president of the old Synagogue in Laederstraede from 1937–1954.

tober 3rd the Danish Lutheran bishops sent an open letter of protest to the German commander in chief and to his troops. In addition, a pastoral letter was read the following Sunday in every church in the country. In part it stated:

> Persecution of the Jews conflicts with the humanitarian conception of the love of neighbors and the message which the church set out to preach.... Persecution conflicts with the judicial conscience existing in the Danish people.... We respect the right to religious worship according to the dictates of conscience.... Notwithstanding our separate religious beliefs we will fight to preserve for our Jewish brothers and sisters the same freedom we ourselves value more than life. The leaders of the Danish church clearly comprehend the duties of law-abiding citizens, but recognize at the same time that they are conscientiously bound to maintain the right and to protest every violation of justice. It is evident that in this case we are obeying God rather than man.[13]

After the reading of the letter, special prayers were said in every church for the safety of Danish Jewry.

On Wednesday afternoon, September 29th, the present writer and his family went to the home of a good Christian friend, C.F. Lerche. Mr. Lerche, a well-known merchant, lived in a three-story house in Gothersgade, Copenhagen. His business was on the main floor, and we settled in on the second floor, occasionally looking out of the window and observing the normal traffic of bicycles and few cars. Six days we stayed here, not knowing what had happened to our family relatives and other fellow Jews. On Tuesday, October 5th, my parents made contact through a "business connection" with a member of the resistance movement, who took us by automobile north to Humlebaek. We were brought to a farmer, who lent his barn to fleeing Jews. In the barn we met many other Danish Jews, all well known to the family. Everybody present had only one thought in mind: How to get to neutral Sweden? The following night, the night between Wednesday and Thursday, Oc-

[13] *Ibid.* p.58

tober 7th and 8th, we left dark Denmark for illuminated Sweden. We belonged to that group which Aage Bertelsen describes in his book *October '43* as the single biggest transport crossing Øresund.

The miraculous flight of the Danish Jews to Sweden has been fully described in other books.[14] The help of the Danes to their Jewish fellow citizens has been praised by all civilized people of the world.

A final word on this writer's personal experience. When my family left our home on Wednesday afternoon, September 29th 1943, it had been prepared for the forthcoming Rosh Hashono holiday. The table was set, candles placed in candlesticks, and the traditional holiday bread baked. When, after twenty-two months, in May 1945, we returned to Copenhagen and reentered our home, everything was exactly as we had left it! The Danes had seen to it that no one entered our home during our absence. Similarly, the Danes watched the synagogues, the Jewish schools, the community center and many Jewish apartments. No looting, stealing or other mischievous acts occurred there.

In all that they did throughout these darkest days of World War II, the Danes remained faithful to their democratic and humanistic tradition. As Harold Flender has written: In Denmark, tradition is the keeper of the flame. When times demanded it, that flame burst forth with a brilliance to warm the heart of mankind. What the Danes did in October, 1943, gave an added meaning to the first lines of the Danish national anthem *Der er et yndigt land, det staar med brede bøge*. Translated, it simply means: "It is a lovely land."

---

[14] Notably, Yad Voshem: Henry Bruun (ed.) *Dansk Historisk Bibliography 1943–1947*, (Copenhagen, 1956); Niels Ebbesen (Aage Heinberg), *Danmark säger Nej*, (Stockholm, 1943); and Ralph Oppenhejm, *Flugten over Øresund*, (Copenhagen, 1946).

The Danish Jews escaped to Sweden via the Øresund.

The Danish Kings

Christian IV	1588 – 1648
Frederick III	1648 – 1670
Christian V	1670 – 1699
Frederick IV	1699 – 1730
Christian VI	1730 – 1746
Frederick V	1746 – 1766
Christian VII	1766 – 1808
Frederick VI	1808 – 1839
Christian VIII	1839 – 1848
Frederick VII	1848 – 1863
Christian IX	1863 – 1906
Frederick VIII	1906 – 1912
Christian X	1912 – 1947
Frederick IX	1947 – 1964
Queen Margarete	1964 –

Rabbis Officiating in Copenhagen

Rabbi Abraham Solomon, 1687 - 1700

Rabbi Israel Behr, 1700 - 1732

Rabbi Marcus David, 1732 - 1736

Rabbi Hirsch Levy, 1741 - 1775

Rabbi Gedalia Levin, 1776 - 1793

Rabbi Abraham Gedalia, 1794 - 1827

Rabbi Abraham Alexander Wolff, 1828 - 1891

Professor David Simonsen, 1891 - 1903

Dr. Tobias Lewenstein, 1903 - 1910

Dr. Max Schornstein, 1910 - 1919

Dr. Max Friediger, 1921 - 1947 (October, 1943 - May, 1945 in Theresienstadt)

Dr. Marcus Melchior, 1947 - 1969

Rabbi Bent Melchior, 1969 - present

Appendix I

To the deputies of the Portuguese nation in Amsterdam
and separately to Hamburg
Dated Haderslev,
the 25th of November 1622

Christian the Fourth

Honorable and especially beloved. We wish to inform you most graciously that since we have graciously learned that various noblemen and masters have asked and desired, in writing, that some of your nation, residing in their areas of juristiction, have considered to settle [there], that he or they present themselves in order to gain further information.

We do consider your nation for our city Glückstadt, not only with all kinds of special privileges, [such as] freedom of religion and commerce, [but] especially to provide yourself according to occasion, and to increase in the future, and suited for amplification. Our servant the mint master and our beloved and trusted Albertus Diony and others will point [this] out to you.

Thus, it is our wish and desire that one or more of your nation, if they lean towards settlement in our city, that one or two persons may of their own accord go there and view the opportunities of the place, in order that they may provide further details. Without doubt they will give you enough satisfaction.

Appendix II

(Translation of Letter)

To The King:
Stockbroker Heiman Levy and grocer Moses Levy, hereby respectfully apply that in the rebuilt synagogue in this city no choir singing may be instituted, no prayers eliminated, shortened or changed, the holy language in no way abbreviated, and no change whatsoever be made in the customs, which from olden times were introduced and used.

The deep sorrow which has overtaken us and our faithful brothers, by the seemingly well substantiated rumors that the laws of Israel be abandoned, and a new sect, directly opposed to our ancient laws, which are supposed to be as God's laws, wish to eliminate prayers, institute choir singing in the language of the land instead of the holy language, has provoked us daringly to approach the throne of your royal majesty, seeking relief for us and our suffering co-religionists.

Through thousands of years, by persecutions and oppressions which we have firmly endured, we have kept these laws with devotion, veneration and love. We have always remained faithful to our religion and its laws. Wise, humane and benevolent rulers with a spirit of justice have granted that we could exercise our religious beliefs and ceremonies in holy peace. Finally, they have obtained citizenship and protection [for us] in the various countries, for which the Almighty bless your majesties and equally minded monarchs.

Throughout Europe it is generally admitted that Israel's customs are religious laws. We are therefore of the opinion, that if the customs are changed, religion is violated. This change cannot serve any purpose. It will degrade the present part of the Jewish generation, which without any motivation seek to destroy the beautiful memory of our people's devotion to God and His laws. They want to rob them of what our forefathers, through numerous sufferings and persecutions, have maintained of its laws and ceremonies. Most gracious King, the majority of members of the Jewish congregation of Copenhagen belong to this group.

We, therefore, most respectfully dare to note that the representatives of the Jewish community here in this city invited its members to donate for the building of the synagogue, which the attached receipts indicate, and by subscribing to these donations [were] by the most honored Dr. Wulff promised that no change would take place at divine services. Should we, your Majesty, who fear God and honor His name, observe with indifferent eyes, that despite these promises, changes are proposed? The treasured object, the ancient formula of prayers, which we have inherited from our forefathers, and which for two thousand years have been transmitted from generation to generation; the order of the service, which is so intensely tied to the spirit of our religion and indivisible from same, should we observe all this encroached upon by anyone, who so would and still remain silent spectators? We have a most gracious king, before whom we can most respectfully submit our complaint, who equally protects religion and people, who will listen to us and alleviate our sorrows.

According to the principle of our religion, prayers are by no means a voluntary act, which can be observed or neglected according to an individual's mood. Prayer is much more than an obligation, which each Jew has to observe equally with other religious obligations.

No consideration in time or space could prevent us from these obligations of which prayers are included. They cannot be changed and are independent of time and circumstances. Guided by these truths, our wise forefathers—the assembly of great men, which included such prophets as Haggai, Zecharia, Malachi, Daniel and their descendants, those men who arranged Mishna and Talmud, authored our prayers and hymns as we now possess—have obligated us to recite these prayers daily, as stated by Maimonides. These divinely inspired men, who gave us their wise decrees and prohibitions, cemented the pillars of our religion, instituted therefore religious services as an essential part of our obligations. These arrangements were unanimously accepted by the entire people, and observed as holy laws and customs. These laws were conscientiously observed as all other religious laws. Two thousand years have passed and these services still exist in their original format. During this great time span, no rabbinical college or assembly have dared to institute a change...

And now, there is one who will dare to extend his hand against this sanctuary! Would this not cause a complete destruction of the status by these divinely inspired men, if someone would suggest the spirit of the time demands it? These laws prohibit: music in the synagogue, any change of the formulas of prayers, elimination of any of them or the holy language.

We furthermore dare, most respectfully, to recall the opinion of your majesty's superintendant general, the learned Adler's consideration in this matter. This consideration we have already submitted in its original to your majesty's Danish chancellery. We permit ourselves to attach a copy. Thus, most gracious king, we and many of our believing co-religionists most respectfully venture to ask protection from any encroachment of our holy religion: no choir singing may be instituted, no prayers eliminated, shortened or changed, the holy language not abolished in any part. Everything shall remain the same way as it has been for two thousand years.

We hope that our most submissive plea will be granted.

In greatest humility

M.Levy
Grocer
S.Pederstraede No.120

Heiman Levy
Stockbroker
Stormgade No. 207

Humbly written and corrected
Jacob Behrendt
Bookprinter
Aabenraae 241

Appendix III

(Ch. XI, Original Leaflet)

OPROP!
Til Danmarks Soldater og Danmarks Folk!

Uten Grund og imot den tyske Regjerings og det tyske Folks oprigtige Ønske, om at leve i Fred og Venskab med det engelske og det franske Folk, har Englands og Frankrigets Magtehavere ifjor i September erklæret Tyskland Krigen.

Deres Hensigt var og blir, efter Mulighed, at treffe Afgjorelser paa Krigsskuepladser som ligger mere afsides og derfor er mindre farlige for Frankriget og England, i det Haab, at det ikke ville være mulig for Tyskland, at kund optræde stærkt nok imot dem.

Af denne Grund har England blandt andet stadig krænket Danmarks og Norges Nøitralitæt og deres territoriale Farvand.

Det forsokte stadig at gjore Skandinavien til Krigsskueplads. Da en yderlig Anledning ikke synes at være givet efter der russisk-finnske Fredsslutning, har man nu officielt erklæret og truct, ikke mere at taale den tyske Handelsflaates Seilads indenfor danske Territorialfarvand ved Nordsjoen og i de norske Farvand. Man erklærte selv at vilde overta Politiopsigten der. Man har tilslut truffet alle Forberedelser for overraskende at ta Besiddelse af alle nodvendige Stotepunkter ved Norges Kyst. Aarhunredes storste Krigsdriver, den allerede i den forst Verdenskrig til Ulykke for hele Menneskeheden arbeidende Churchill, uttalte det aapent, at han ikke var villig til at la sig holde tilbake af "legale Afgjorelser eller noitrale Rettigheder som staar paa Papirlapper".

Han har forberedt Slaget mot den danske og den norske Kyst. For nogen Daget siden er han blit utnævnt til foransvarlig Chef for hele den britiske Krigsføring.

154

Den tyske Regjering har til nu overvaaket denne Mands Forholdsregler, men den kan ikke taale, at en ny Krikssueplads nur blir skaffet efter de engelsk-franske Krigsdriveres Ønsker.

Den danske og den norske Regjering har siden Maaneder hat Beskjed om disse Forsøk.

Likeledes er deres Holdning ingen Hemmelighed for den tyske Regjering. De er hverken villige eller istand til at kunne yde en virksom Motstand mot det engelske Indbrudd.

Derfor har Tyskland beslutte at foregripe det engelske Angrep og med sine Magtmidler selv at overta Beskyttelsen av Danmarks og Norges Kongeriges Nøitraliotæt og værne den saalænge Krigen varer.

Det er ikke den tyske Regjerings Hensigt at skaffe sig et Støttepunkt i Kampen mot England, den har udelukkende det Maal at forhindre at Skandinavien blir Slagmark for de engelske Krigsudvidelser.

Af denne Grund har stærke tyske Militærkræfter siden idag morges tat Besiddelse af de vigtigste militære Objekter i Danmark og Norge. Over disse Forholdsregler treffes der for Tiden Overenskomster mellem den tyske Riksregjering og den Kongelige Danske Regjering. Disse Overenskomster skal sikre at Kongeriget bestaar videre, at Hæren og Flaaten opretholdes, at det Danske Folks Frihet agtes og at dette Lands fremtidige Uafhængighed fuldt ut sikres.

Indtil disse Forhandlinger er afsluttet, maa der ventes at Hæren og Flaaten har Forstaaelse for dette, likeledes at Folket og alle kommunale Seder er fornuftige og har god Vilje, slik at de undlater enhver passiv eller aktiv Motstand. Den vilde være uten Nytte og bli brudt med alle Magtmidler. Alle militære og kommunale Steder anmodes derfor straks at opta Forbindelsen med de tyske Kommandører.

Folket opfordres til at fortsætte det daglige Arbeide og til at sørge for Rolighed og Orden!

For Landets Sikkerhet mod engelske Overgrep sørger fra nu af den tyske Hær og Flaade.

            Den Tyske Kommandør
               Kaupisch

Chief Rabbi Max Friediger and Dr. Marcus Melchior at Scandinavian Jewish Youth Organization Congress, c. 1937

Julius Margolinsky, Nov. 19, 1895–Feb. 9, 1978
(Picture by Jerry Bergman)

Helene Perlstein, d. 1901

Bibliography

Abrahams, Beth Zion. *The Life of Glückel of Hameln*. New York: Horovitz Publishing Co., 1963.

Altschul, Simon. *Di Geshichte Fun Di Yuden in Denemark*. København: Dos Wochenblat, 1921.

Baar, Jacob and Cahnman, Werner J. (ed.) *Intermarriage and Jewish Life*. New York: The Herzl Press, 1963.

Balslev, Benjamin. *De Danske Jøders Historie*. København: O. Lohse, 1932.

Behr, Israel. *Ohel Yisroel*. Zolkiev: Chayim David ben Aaron, 1802.

Bertelsen, Aage. *October '43*. New York: P.G. Putman's Sons, 1954.

Borchsenius, Poul. *Historien om de Danske Jøder*. København: Fremad, Det Hoffenbergske Establissement, 1969.

Borum, O.A. *Dansk Lovsamling (1665 - 1891)*. København: G.E.C. Gads Forlag, 1931.

Borup, Morton. *Breve far og til Holger Drachman*. København: Gyldendals - Nordisk Forlag, 1970.

_____. *Meir Goldschmidt's Breve til Hans Familie*. København: Rosenkilde og Bagger, 1964.

Brandes, Georg. *Samlede Skrifter*. København: Gyldendalske Boghandels Forlag, 1899.

Bredsdorff, Elias. *Corsaren*. København: Carit Andersen Forlag, 1941.

Caro, Joseph, *Shulchan Aruch-Choshen Mishpot*. Amsterdam: Emanuel ben Joseph Atiash. 1699.

Christensen, Villads. *Peripatetikeren Søren Kierkegaard*. København: Graabrødre Torv's Forlag, 1965.

Cohen, A.D. *De Mosaiske Troesbekjeneres Stilling i Danmark*. Odense: 1837.

Colding Jørgensen, H. *Sàertryk af Nationaløkonomisk Tidskrift.* København: 1934.
Collected Works of Voltaire. New York: Greystone Press, 1948.
Denmark: *The Constitution or Fundamental Law for the Kingdom of Denmark.* Christiansted, St. Croix, no date.
Edelmann, Raphael. "David Simonsen." *Ved 150 Aarsdagen for Anordningen af 29 Marts, 1814.* Det Mosaiske Troessamfund København: A/S Oscar Fraenkel, 1964.
Federation of Jewish Philantrophies, Commission of Synagogue Relations. Proceedings of a Conference: *Intermarriage and the Future of the American Jew.* New York: December 1964.
Fischer, Josef. *Slaegten Levin-Fredericia.* København: A/S Oscar Fraenkel's Bogtrykkeri, 1916.

---. "Prof. D. Simonsen's Literaere Publikationer." *Festskrift i Anledning af Professor David Simonsen 70-aarige Fødselsdag.* København: Hertz Bogtrykkeri, 1923.

---. "Prof. D. Simonsen's Vorfahren." *Festskrift i Anledning af Professor David Simonsen's 70-aarige Fødselsdag.* København: Hertz Bogtrykkeri, 1923.

Flender, Harold. *Rescue in Denmark.* New York: Macfadden-Bartell Corporation, 1964.
Friediger, Max. *Jødernes Historie.* København: P. Haase & Søns Forlag, 1934.
Fortegnelser over Legater tilligemed de for disse Legater Gjaeldende Fundatser. København: O.C. Olsen & Co., 1878.
Tillaeg 1890
Tillaeg II 1903
Goldschmidt, M.À. *Samlede Vàerker.* København: Gyldendalske Boghandel-Nordisk Forlag, 1909.
Gottlob, A. *Andagtsbog for Israeliter.* København: H.C. Brille Officin, 1843.
Hagensen, A. *Den Jødiske Periode, 1864 - 1900.* København: E. Jespersons Forlag, 1901.
Hartman, Grethe and Schulsinger, Fini. *Physical and Mental Stress and Consequential Development of Atherosclorosis within the Jewish Population of Denmark.* Copenhagen: Rosenkilde and Bagger, 1952.
Hartvig, Michael. *Jøderne i Danmark i Tiden 1600 - 1800.* København: G.E.C.Gads Forlag, 1951.
Himmelstrup, Jens og Møller, Jens. *Danske Forfatningslove.* København: J.H. Schutz Forlag, 1958.

Horin, Ben Meir. "Intermarriage and the Survival of the Jewish People." *Intermarriage and Jewish Life*. New York: The Herzl Press, 1963.

Kalkar, Nathan Simon. *N'teay Shashuim*. København: 1834.

Krüger, Paul (ed.) *Correspondence of G. Brandes*. Copenhagen: Rosenkilde og Bagger, 1956.

Linvald, Steffen. "Den Jødiske Frihedskamp i Danmark og Anordningen af 29 Marts 1814," *Ved 150 Aars-Dagen for Anordningen af 29 Marts 1814*. Det Mosaiske Troessamfund. København: A/S Oscar Fraenkel, 1964.

Margolinsky, Julius (ed.) *Chevra Kaddischa 1858 - 1958*. København: A/S Oscar Fraenkel, 1958.

——————. (ed.) *Danmark Loge, U.O.B.B. No. 712*. København: A/S Oscar Fraenkel, 1962.

——————. "Det Jødiske Folketal i Danmark efter 1814." *Ved 150 Aars-Dagen for Anondningen af 29 Marts 1814*. Det Mosaiske Troessamfund. København: A/S Oscar Fraenkel, 1964.

——————. *Ligfølgeselskabet - Jødiske Broderselskab af 1768*. København: B. Nielsen's Eftf. 1967.

——————. *Omkring Fadderselskabet's 150 Aars Jubilaeum*. København: 1960.

——————. *Statistiske Undersøgelser over Alders og Kønsfordeling m.m. blandt Flygtninge fra Danmark*. Stockholm: 1945.

Meisels, Abraham Nathan Nota, Rabbi. *Shagas Arye v'Kol Schachal*. Saloniki: 1746.

Melchior, Marcus. "1943-1953," *Ved 150 Aars-Dagen of Anordningen af 29 Marts 1814*. Det Mosaiske Troessamfund. København: A/S Oscar Fraenkel, 1964.

Meyer, Poul. "Gudstjenesten i Brydningstiden efter 1814." *Ved 150 Aars-Dagen for Anordningen af 29 Marts 1814*. Det Mosaiske Troessamfund. København: A/S. Oscar Fraenkel, 1964.

Moritzen, Julius. *Georg Brandes in Life and Letters*. Newark: D.S. Colyer, 1922.

Nakman, Hillel. "Et lille jødisk Tidsbillede fra Haveforeningerne 'Taga' og 'Lilgen.'" *Ved 150 Aars-Dagen for Anordningen af 29 Marts 1814*. Det Mosaiske Troessamfund København: A/S Oscar Fraenkel, 1964.

Nathansen, Henri. *Georg Brandes - Et Portráet*. København: Nyt Nordisk Forlag, 1929.

Nathanson, M.L. *Historisk Fremstilling af Jødernes Forhold og Stilling i Danmark*. København: Berlingske Bogtrykkeri, 1860.
Nolin, Bertil. *Den Gode Europén*. Uppsala: Almqvist och Wiksells, 1965.
Rubin, Marcus. "En ikke offentliggjordt Afhandling-Den Jødiske Befolkning i København 1885." *Ved 150 Aars-Dagen for Anordningen af 29 Marts 1814*. Det Mosaiske Troessamfund. København: A/S Oscar Fraenkel, 1964.
Salomon, Julius. *Bidrag til Dansk Jødisk Historie 1820 - 1845*. København: O.C. Olsen & Co., 1903.
_____. *Eheschliessungen zwichen Juden und Christen in Kopenhagen in den Jahren 1880 - 1903*. Zeitschrift für Demographie und Statistik der Juden. Berlin: 1905.
Salomon, Julius og Fischer, Josef. *Mindeskrift i Anledning af Hundredaarsdagen for Anordningen af 29 Marts 1814*. Kjøbenhavn: J. Jørgensen & Co., 1914.
Trap, Cordt. *Russische Juden in Kopenhagen*. Zeitschrift für Demographie und Statistik der Juden, Neue Folge. Berlin: 1926.
Wahrman, M. *Samling af Bønner til Brug ved den første Undervisning i Hebraisk*. København: H.E. Kleins Forlag, 1848.
Werner, Johannes. *Gedalia og hans Forfáedre*. København: H. Hirschprungs Forlag, 1933.
Wolff, A.A. *Agende for det Mosaiske Troessamfunds Synagogue København*. København: 1833.
Yad Vashem. *Best-Sagen*, Copenhagen Municipal Court, Proceedings of the Danish Supreme Court. C.E. Gad, 1950.
Zeitschrift für Demographie und Statistik der Juden. Berlin: Vol. 1 - 3, 1905 - 1907.
_____. *Neue Folge 1 - 3*. Berlin: 1924 - 1926.

Articles and Periodicals

Arnheim, Arthur. "Den Jødiske Menighed i København." *Jødisk Samfund.* Jan., Feb., March, 1950.

Billed Bladet. *Berlinske Tidende.* June 19, 1945.

Bredsdorff, Elias. "Georg Brandes as a Fictional Character in Some Danish Novels and Plays," *Scandinavian Studies* Volume 45 (Winter 1973), Number 1.

Lund, Jens. "The Legend of the King and the Star." *Indiana Folklore* Volume VIII, Number 1-2, 1975.

Margolinsky, Julius. "Jødiske Blade i Danmark." *Jødisk Samfund,* 1954.

Tidskrift for Jødisk Historie og Litterature. Vol. I, II, III. København: 1919 – 1925.

Unpublished Material

Levy, Moses. Letter to the Danish King, June 1832.

Margolinsky, Julius. "Urtekráemmer Moses Levy og hans Synagogue i Láederstraede" Address delivered to Danmark Logen, Jan. 8, 1957.